"What a great book! Monte has ca.... ing your children in ways that draw them to the Lord. His parents' wonderful marriage, his childhood, and the raising of his children were filled with great examples to teach me how I can woo my children into a love relationship that points them to Christ."

"Monte Swan is a great conversationalist. I can tell you without reservation—this is a book you ought to read. Swan has written wisely and well on the lost art of nurturing children. This book focuses on authority that is kind, whose easy yoke and light burden bring rest to the soul. *Romancing Your Child's Heart* will make you a better spouse, friend, brother, sister, and most of all a better parent."

"*Romancing Your Child's Heart* provides a refreshing reminder that the consistent administration of pure love to a child's heart is still the key to real success in parenting."

"If out of all the multitudinous books on parenting out there, we were told that parents could choose but one—this would be the one. Were all new parents to read it, America would be a different place. I just wish I could have read it forty years ago! How many things I would have done differently!"

"This book is the first incision for a parental pharisee-ectomy. As parents, we are so often frightened into judging our children by exterior standards and timetables that we forget that they are a treasure from God and they are okay just the way He has formed them. Monte dares us to love and enjoy our children with all the freedom and wide-open spaces that Christ has called us to live in."

KATHERINE VON DUYKE, MOTHER

"This engaging book looks at the family and sees it whole, looks at love and finds it boundlessly creative. There is a vision here—sorely needed in our overloaded and resentful homes—of freedom, adventure, and delight. *Romancing Your Child's Heart* recaptures the joy of raising children by transforming training and instruction—both biblical ideas—into a lifelong courtship."

RICHARD A. SWENSON, PHYSICIAN
AND AUTHOR OF *MARGIN* AND *THE OVERLOAD SYNDROME*

"Monte Swan has written an encouraging and creative book for parents, filled with practical ideas on how to fill our kids with joy and love rather than guilt and obligation. All parents will be profited by this helpful and insightful book."

JAY KESLER, CHANCELLOR OF TAYLOR UNIVERSITY

"Monte's life and his book are great reminders to me that my greatest calling is not preaching the gospel to thousands sitting in big church buildings, but being Christ's gospel to my kids as we hunt for crawdads in the ditch. May this book assist you in loving your children, and even more—may it help you to see how you are a child being romanced to life by the living God."

PETER HIETT, SENIOR PASTOR OF
LOOKOUT MOUNTAIN COMMUNITY CHURCH, GOLDEN, COLORADO

# ROMANCING YOUR CHILD'S HEART

## MONTE SWAN

### with Dr. David Biebel

Multnomah® Publishers *Sisters, Oregon*

ROMANCING YOUR CHILD'S HEART
published by Multnomah Publishers, Inc.
© 2002 by Monte Swan and David Biebel

International Standard Book Number: 1-59052-280-X

Published in Association with Loyal Arts Literary Agency, LoyalArts.com.

Cover image by Getty Images/EyeWire Collection
Interior design by Katherine Lloyd, The DESK, Bend, Oregon

Chapter epigraphs are from the author's songs.
Unless otherwise indicated, Scripture quotations are from:
*The Holy Bible,* New King James Version
© 1984 by Thomas Nelson, Inc.

Other Scripture quotations are from:
*The Holy Bible,* New International Version (NIV)
© 1973, 1984 by International Bible Society,
used by permission of Zondervan Publishing House

Grateful acknowledgment is made to The CS Lewis Company Ltd
for permission to use material from the following works of C. S. Lewis:
*The Last Battle,* by C. S. Lewis copyright © C. S. Lewis Pte. Ltd. 1956.
*The Screwtape Letters,* by C. S. Lewis copyright © C. S. Lewis Pte. Ltd. 1942.
*On Stories and Other Essays,* by C. S. Lewis copyright © C. S. Lewis Pte. Ltd. 1981.
*They Stand Together,* by C. S. Lewis copyright © C. S. Lewis Pte. Ltd. 1979.
Extracts reprinted by permission.

*Multnomah* is a trademark of Multnomah Publishers, Inc., and is registered in the U.S. Patent
and Trademark Office. The colophon is a trademark of Multnomah Publishers, Inc.

Printed in the United States of America

For information:
MULTNOMAH PUBLISHERS, INC.
POST OFFICE BOX 1720
SISTERS, OREGON 97759

Library of Congress Cataloging-in-Publicaiton Data

Swan, Monte.
    Romancing your child's heart / by Monte Swan with David Biebel.
        p. cm.
    Includes bibliographical references.
    ISBN 1-59052-280-X (pbk.)
    1. Swan, Monte.  2. Christian biography.  3. Parent and child—Religious aspects—
Christianity. I. Biebel, David.  II. Title.

BR1725.S88A3 2003
248.8'45--dc21

                                                                              2003006572
                03 04 05 06 07 08—10 9 8 7 6 5 4 3 2

*To my wonderful parents,*
*Emery and Betty Swan.*

*Your lives wrote this book.*

# Contents

# Acknowledgments

Peter Hiett, my pastor: Much of this book flowed from your messages. They broke spiritual dams while anchoring me biblically and helped me see the Larger Story and the romance more clearly.

Dr. David Biebel: Without you, my friend, brother, and fellow archer, this book could not have been written. In reality, I sang melody and you sang harmony.

Thanks to: Matt Jacobson, for believing in this vision and being my friend.

Thomas Womack, Michael Christopher, and Margaret Sharpe, who took what was a pearly Colorado sky and turned it into a clear blue Colorado sky.

Kathy von Duyke and Tia Ciferno, for the continual prayer and encouragement and deep creative thought they gave throughout my research and writing.

Wade and Jessica Hulcy and the KONOS family, for their moral support and kindred-spiritship as I began this project.

Dr. Joe Wheeler, who helped me strengthen my idea of story: It is an honor to know you.

Stan Keith, for challenging my ideas and preventing me from taking myself too seriously.

Those who read my manuscript or discussed the idea of romance at various stages, encouraging me to write this book, including: Gene Swanson, Bruce Cripe, Jodi Hogle, Jim and Marty Johnson, Bekki Anderson, Philip Yancey, Ray and Trish Cone, Kevin Keating, Levinia Hayes, Gina Braun, Laurie

Bailey, Bob and Tina Farewell, Chris McCluskey, Chuck Bolte, Vicky Goodchild, Gayle Graham, Dr. Larry Crabb, Dave and Joan Exley, Dr. Tedd Tripp, Bob Cryder, Dr. Ruth Beechick, Lisa Jacobson, Carol Bartley, and all the others who have sat around our dining room table.

My brothers and sisters-in-law: Mike and Linda, Skip and Cindy, and Scott and Chris. I am sure you are what God envisioned when He imagined family.

Heather, Travis, and Dawson, for your unconditional love, and for gladly giving Papa permission to use you as illustrations.

And Karey, the "fairest of ten thousand." You are my coauthor.

# Straight and True

*He was an arrow in our quiver,*
*Then we held him in our hand.*
*Soon the bowstring held the arrow,*
*And the aiming part began.*

"High and Far"

For as long as I can remember I've been enchanted by the flight of an arrow. By age four, inspired by legends of heroic archers in days gone by whose fame would live forever, I was making my own bows from alders by the creek and arrows from the straightest sticks I could find. From my mother's sewing cabinet I smuggled strings for my bows and pieces of cloth to make a proper archer's attire.

Even today, when I pick up a bow, I'm transported back to the woods behind our home in Wisconsin, where I was Robin Hood leading his Merry Men. I can see the green leaves of springtime, smell the flowers of summer and the burning leaves of autumn as I crawl along the musty earth, trying to ambush one of the king's deer or anything else with fur or feathers. Though I never hit a single bird or beast, my joy was undiminished because I was living a fairy tale, participating in a story in which the adventure was everything. My boyish soul was caught up in the romance of it all.

Early one morning when my children were still young, I arose before dawn. Life felt wonderful, just as it had when I was a child. But adult anxiety suddenly gripped me. I want this day to last forever. I wish time would slow down! I have these arrows in my quiver, but before they can be released they need to be sharpened, fletched, balanced, maybe even straightened.

With these thoughts in my head I sat down and penned a song I called "Arrows." The chorus went like this:

*And time seems to fly*
*Oh, the years pass so quickly now,*
*Like sand through your fingers*
*You hold it once and then it's gone.*
*The children keep changin'.*
*They grow as the years rush by.*
*Like arrows in a quiver,*
*They're made to someday fly.*[1]

More recently, when our oldest son joined my wife, Karey, and me in singing for a group of parents, it suddenly struck me: The future has arrived. Travis was already a college student, a balanced arrow, strong and sharp. But which way would he fly? How straight? How true?

When we finished, the audience wanted to question Travis, something we hadn't anticipated or rehearsed. They weren't as interested in our advice as they were in knowing how our approach had worked with a real person!

Karey and I stood behind our son, waiting for our report card to be read in public. The suspense was intense; all we could do was watch, listen, and pray.

"Do you feel your parents oversheltered you as you grew up?"

"Not at all," Travis replied. "I didn't feel so much sheltered as strengthened."

Travis's response brought me face-to-face with a reality that eventually confronts every parent. One day our child is safe in the quiver; then we hold the arrow in our hands; and the next day the arrow is on the string, the bow is bent, and the child is released and flying into the future toward some target beyond us. Much of the flight we will not even be around to see.

Our hope is that our child will fly straight and true to the heart of Jesus. Yet most of us have known sincere Christian parents who lost their child's heart. They've watched as sons or daughters turn their backs on God and walk away—their love and affection captured by the world. These parents may have diligently tried to protect their children from evil and prepare them for success in life. They may have taught them biblical doctrine and trained them in proper Christian behavior. But the children chose the way of fools—the way of wickedness. It doesn't make sense, and we desperately hope it won't happen to us.

Perhaps protection, preparation, and even Christian training and biblical knowledge are not the real keys. Maybe these valid and essential things can monopolize too much of our time, distracting us from the real issue—the winning of our child's heart.

While we're guarding the front door, is it possible Satan is sneaking in the back? Could there be a missing ingredient in today's parenting model, something of which even the most committed Christian parents may be unaware, yet something that will guard that back door?

I believe there is.

The key to winning the hearts of our children is the often overlooked biblical concept of romance—not the world's concept, but God's. He sent Jesus Christ to earth not to storm our hearts but to woo us and draw us to Himself, winning our uncompelled love. If we truly make Him our model, and pattern our approach to our children after His approach to us, we automatically begin to parent from the inside out instead of the outside in. We look past behavior to the heart; we look past symptoms to the cause; we turn isolated events into shared, romance-enhancing experiences that connect to something larger than ourselves.

How exactly a child's heart-desires turn to God we don't know. But we do know the Holy Spirit gives that desire and we parents are used as instruments of God in this process.

*Romancing Your Child's Heart* builds on the belief that romance is central to the biblical parenting model. It presents a vision that will help us reexamine and reassess whole realms of our lives.

Why? Because nothing is more important for parents than winning our child's heart for Christ.

Part One:

# ROMANCING YOUR CHILD
## ~ THE VISION ~

*I see His blood upon the rose,*
*And in the stars the glory of His eyes.*
*His body gleams amid eternal snows;*
*His tears fall from the skies.*
*I see His face in every flower;*
*The thunder and the singing of the birds*
*Are but His voice—and, carven by His power*
*Rocks are His written words.*
*All pathways by His feet are worn,*
*His strong heart stirs the ever-beating sea,*
*His crown of thorns is twined with every thorn,*
*His cross is every tree.*

JOSEPH M. PLUNKETT

# Chapter 1

# Once upon a Childhood

*He's found riches in rocks and ropes and rain*
*And in bugs and bark and bones.*
*He's got a treasure trove that money can't buy*
*And his own gold mine in his boyhood blue sky.*

"Fires of His Wonder"

Once upon a time a little boy lived in the north woods of Wisconsin.

He lived in a log cabin, built decades after the last stands of virgin white pines had all been logged. Homesteaders had followed, but by the time of the boy's birth most of them had moved elsewhere. Abandoned homesteads and overgrown fields whispered tales of hard labor and lean times, of the courage of those who struggled to cultivate this land of stony soil and short summers.

The boy's grandfather, the son of Swedish immigrants, told him many stories of those early days "when da pines gruew so tall dat da highest branches seemed to vreach da stars, and vhen you valked amoung dem it vas like valking truew a catedral."

Sometimes the old man's voice quavered with emotion. A faraway look in his gray blue eyes pulled the boy in, and suddenly he would be there, in the story with his grandfather, wandering through an enchanted forest created by God.

The cabin symbolized his parents' dream of establishing a simple home in a beautiful place, close to nature and family. It stood at the edge of a deep, clear lake, seven miles from town on a country road that wound through hardwood hills and scented cedar swamps. It included a porch for sitting and a fireplace sculpted of fieldstones from the rock pile of an abandoned homestead. The forest surrounding it possessed a timeless serenity that stilled the souls of all who passed by.

> *The boy never forgot what that stump said to his soul in that magical moment.*

Diamonds danced on the waters of summer. The lake was also alive with fish, which the boy's mother loved to catch. One sunny day, when the boy was three, his mother returned from the lake holding up a stringer of bass. She claimed she could set her watch by those bass, which fed every day at the same time. The boy's father came down to see, but when they turned to show her catch to their son, he had disappeared.

They thought first of the lake, but it was calm. They looked in the cabin. They scanned the woods, where the sanctuary of dark green hemlock and cedar, roots entwined, had grown into a maze that almost blocked their way.

Just as they were about to plunge in, they saw the boy sitting on the soft moss at the edge of the trees, trying to hug the ancient, charred stump of a white pine. He was making friends, using all his senses to study this sentry of the woods. He was a "tree hugger" before tree hugging was cool.

The boy never forgot how that stump smelled, felt, tasted,

or even what it said directly to his soul in that magical moment—a story of the million hours of sunlight it had drunk in, of primeval land that had never felt the blade of a plow or heard the ring of an ax. Someone was wooing his heart. He was in a state of pure wonder.

As you've probably guessed, that boy was me. Looking back, it seems both poetic and prophetic that this—my earliest memory—involves God's romancing my heart to Himself. My parents never forgot that day, and in the years to follow they often recalled that picture of their son's first true encounter with God's creation.

## LIKE THE NORTH STAR

After the old-growth hemlock and hardwoods of northern Wisconsin had been logged off, my father found work in the carpentry trade in southern Wisconsin. But we frequently returned "up north" to visit my grandfather's cabin, trips that I anticipated with such passion that thoughts of them occupied my mind for days.

In the summer I often stayed for extended periods with Grandpa. Life was simple there, mostly revolving around fishing, swimming, exploring, and storytelling. My grandfather told story upon story, connecting me to the old days. Our imaginations fed off each other. We were friends, roaming from place to place, each story leading to another, nurturing and reinforcing my sense of wonder. I wanted to know all about the trees, the fish, and my great-grandfather's world.

I was often homesick during my stays with Grandpa, but

my experiences with him reinforced my passion for the outdoors—especially fishing for muskies, the "fish of three
thousand casts." (By the time I was twelve, I had a severe case
of "muskie fever," and my parents helped me start a business
delivering newspapers so I could feed
my fever; it took me a year and a half
to save enough money to buy the specialized equipment I needed.)

> *The crick held
> a mystical quality
> unlike anything I'd
> known before.*

When each stay with Grandpa
ended and it was time to go south
again, tears filled my eyes as I watched
the last of the old pine stumps disappear into the distance.
The stumps were monuments to paradox—on one hand, they
spoke of creation, beauty, and nature; on another, of greed,
fire, and civilization. They were my link to the old times, a special bond I shared with those who had gone before.

As I grew older, "up north" became a reference point, like
the North Star, helping me regain my orientation when life
didn't seem to make sense. Recently, while visiting my parents,
I searched for just one stump to show my son. I soon realized
they're all gone.

## MY MYSTICAL TUTOR

In southern Wisconsin where we moved, my father had built
another house for his family, next to a stream I called the
"crick."

The crick drew me with irresistible force. It held a mys-
tical quality unlike anything I'd known before. Beyond the

flowing water, which would have called to any boy my age, the stream possessed an identity of its own. Its face changed with each new day; every changing season provided newly penned stories, written just for me.

At first, my parents didn't allow me to go near it. The waters seemed dangerous even if they were quite shallow. But before long they realized it was in my best interest to begin my "schooling" there. For several years the crick tutored me in biology and geology as well as engineering and architecture.

I constructed dams of rocks and mud that would some-times stop the flow of water long enough for me to run downstream and collect fish and crawdads. I also built a tree house above the crick, complete with an intricate network of rope swings. While I was hammering on it one day, the main supports broke and everything fell. I did a full gainer and ended up sticking my head into the mud three feet under water. I swallowed about a quart of water before figuring out which way was up and finding the surface. But that challenge was nothing compared to my mother's efforts to empty my stomach and clean me up.

I captured many creatures in or near the crick to keep as pets. My favorites were baby snapping turtles and little fish—one of which my youngest brother eventually trained to jump into his hand. I kept salamanders in our basement, in a hole near two well pipes. They liked the arrangement so much they made it a family affair, reproducing until there were nearly a dozen, all living a lizard's utopian dream. They waited patiently for me to feed them the juicy night crawlers I gathered after summer rains. And though my mother dreaded walking across that section of the basement to get to the root cellar, she never asked me to remove the creatures, or my father to cement the hole.

One day, Mom found fishing worms floating to the surface in her washing machine. I'd figured out that my jeans pockets were the best place to carry angleworms, which I dug as I fished. After the initial shock she laughed and laughed. Later, though, she shed a tear or two as she realized that someday there would no longer be fish bait floating in her wash, and she would miss the child who had grown up.

I developed a taste for the wild berries and apples that grew near the crick, though as a botanist in training I was often more interested in studying than in eating them. The black raspberries seemed like miraculous treasures created just for me. It was hard to imagine how God could pack so much juice and joy into such a tiny package. I once came across some and, without eating even one, picked them and carried them to my mother in a pouch made of a once-white T-shirt. Instead of scolding me, she thanked me for my generosity— then got me a berry bucket.

I repossessed many rafts, skiffs, and canoes left abandoned in the field behind our place by the spring runoff, and floated them down the crick, ducking bridges and balancing precariously as I ran minirapids.

A rock hound neighbor, noticing my passion for nature, planted wonderful mineral and fossil specimens along the crick for me to find and collect. These "discoveries" ignited the flames that later fueled my interest in geology and led to my life's work.

Only when I became a man did I realize God is like that neighbor, hiding treasures for us to find as He draws us to

Himself. And wise and blessed are the parents who help their children find them.

## FREEDOM TO EXPLORE

The budding geologist in me dug underground forts. In each "dig" I measured and recorded the various soil layers and longed to read the story behind the stratigraphic record. Once, after intersecting a layer of pure gray clay, I sculpted every type of dinosaur known at the time and exhibited these works of art on the front porch of our house. This didn't exactly match my mother's decorating scheme, but she swallowed hard and even praised the gooey display.

In autumn, as the leaves began to fall and the Winesap apples cured to a rich flavor, I became a little pioneer, wandering farther and farther each year, following the crick both upstream and down. One year, in a grove of huge hardwoods, I discovered a tree house so high it took my breath away. The image of that enchanted tower, and so many other experiences like it, fueled my imagination. I spun dozens of yarns for my mother and father, who always listened as if they'd never heard such tales before.

*My parents had seen how the vast beauty of nature mesmerized me.*

In winter the crick became a wonderland. The young physicist in me was fascinated by the transformation of water to ice and back again. I would lie on it, slide on it, jump on it, always trying to know it more intimately. Early in the winter I saw fish through the ice and chased them up and down the stream. When the water froze solid I sometimes skated for miles, jumping logs and sliding down frozen rapids.

One winter afternoon, the ice broke beneath me in a large sheet, throwing me headlong into the water. It was ten degrees below zero, so my clothes froze immediately. To my surprise, this insulated me from the cold. Excited by this discovery, I ran all the way home with my nearly frozen dog beside me. As I marched through the doorway, my parents said I looked like a knight in transparent armor. They ignored the dripping water as they listened to my tale of yet another adventure.

My parents had seen how the vast and lush beauty of nature mesmerized me, so they gave me freedom to explore it. I know now it was God drawing me to Himself. I became intimate with the work of God's hands, and this made me desire to know Him.

## BRINGING OUT THE BOY

This magical, adventurous childhood seemed to go on forever, until I turned seven and had to go to school. After just three days I was already lost in a wilderness of vowels, consonants, and rules. The Dick and Jane primers told no tales like those I had read in the trees and rocks. My body, accustomed to constant motion, desperately wanted to escape.

Only the respect for authority I'd learned from my parents held me there. I watched the giant wall clock, and the strain began to show. I developed embarrassing facial tics that could be controlled only through concentrated effort. When I tried to read, my mind wandered. My eyes focused on the farthest horizon outside the window, which connected me to the crick, and beyond that to Grandpa's cabin up north, where I most yearned to be.

Teachers thought I was willfully daydreaming as I stared out the windows. But the real issue was a problem with my eyes. Though I had exceptional vision, when I looked at pages of words I saw double. My brain had to force the letters to come together, causing painful neurological fatigue. The only relief I had came from gazing at the far horizon. Years later an eye doctor diagnosed this condition as a simple convergent problem that could have been corrected had it been noticed earlier.

I compensated for my reading difficulty by putting great energy into show-and-tell and special projects, especially science- and art-oriented projects, in which I excelled. During these years, my parents went out of their way to support my ideas, and most of all to believe in me. I responded so well to their encouragement that they were unaware of my struggles.

Two teachers in fourth and fifth grades took a special interest in me. They seemed to understand. One gave me classroom time to pursue my projects; the other spent many hours reading books such as The Mysterious Island aloud to the class. This hooked me on the power of books, and to everyone's surprise, I began to read passionately.

Years later, I found a kindred spirit in the dedication of Charles Pellegrino's spellbinding archaeological book, *Unearthing Atlantis:*

To five who believed in a "retarded" boy who could not read, but thought he would. Mom, Dad, Adelle,

Barbara, and Dennis, thank you for not believing in test scores, for not browbeating and for believing instead that you could bring the boy out by encouraging his love of science.[2]

## STRATEGIC LOVE

Two teachers who believed in me, two loving parents, and the wonders of creation were God's instruments as He orchestrated a romance with a stressed-out, reading-impaired, hard-to-educate, dreaming-designing-digging-sculpting-building boy with crick mud on his britches.

My parents continued to love me strategically through my adolescent years, when it became more challenging and complex. They knew they couldn't protect me from the temptations teenagers face, so their strategy was simply to out-romance the competition rather than build a wall around me.

> *God orchestrated a romance with a stressed-out boy with crick mud on his britches.*

They continued to provide me as many options as possible to discover my talents, gifts, and natural inclinations. Whether this involved science, music, art, cooking, fashion, car buying, or athletics, they went the extra mile to ensure I would find the expression of God's creative image within. They nourished my dreams, aspirations, and visions by protecting and cultivating my creativity. And when they encouraged me to design, to bring order from disorder, and to make things, I sensed a camaraderie with my Creator.

Mom and Dad might not have been the perfect models of today's parenting manuals, but the freedom they gave both to me and to my three brothers, within certain well-defined limits, expressed their respect for us as individuals and earned our lifelong devotion. I know now they won our hearts through the irresistible force of their sacrificial love.

Although their life together included its share of adversity and tragedy, they continued to trust God and press on, protecting us with a hedge of hope and joy and a genuine vision for God's Larger Story. Their unconditional love and grace and their faith in me quenched any rebellion before it arose in my heart.

My mom, on reading this manuscript, said, "Monte, you enlarged what we did."

"Of course," I told her. "I was looking for the Larger Story."

My parents gave me a safe place to grow—a home where fairy tales really did come true.

And I believe that all of us—by using God's creation and encouraging creative activities, while providing the security of unconditional love—can do the same for our own children.

Chapter 2

# Finding the Silver Bullet

*When she was just a little girl,*
*She'd dream of days gone by,*
*Of dashing Prince Charmings,*
*And castles in the sky;*
*Of a story told untold times,*
*Romantic words of love,*
*A haunting strain sung again,*
*A dance from above.*

"Is This Romance?"

One summer in my boyhood, I made seven dollars by working three days to whitewash an Oscar Mayer stock pen. I invested my entire pay not in candy or even fishing gear, but in a book entitled *Prehistoric America.* It described how the discipline of geology began. I read it myself, then my mother read it aloud to me. My fascination with this book, added to the rocks I found along the crick, was the beginning of my career as a geologist. Mom was as interested in the earth as I was, and sharing that book gave us a bond I treasure to this day.

Seeing this new passion in me, Mom and Dad took me to

museums, lectures, and even on a family trip through the Rocky Mountains. Mom once arranged for me to meet with a paleontologist to help me conduct a carbon-14 test for a science fair. The scientist, delighted that I would attempt such a project, generously supplied me with a piece of a mastodon tusk and some ancient charcoal from an anthropological dig. Although the experiment produced little more than some pure white smoke, it took first place in the science fair and started me thinking seriously about science as a career.

Years later, as a sophomore in college, I switched my major from civil engineering to my childhood love, geology. As I studied this field, I became more and more enthralled with the idea of moving "out west," where rocks are well-exposed. Mom and Dad encouraged me to go, though it meant I would be living far away from them. They knew that my love for God's creation, adventure in the mountains, and my chosen profession were all calling me.

For ten years I roamed the western United States, four-wheeling and backpacking in search of gold, copper, zinc, and uranium. It was a life filled with startling beauty, breathtaking vistas, and high adventure. There was my first desert hike into the Superstition Wilderness without water, and the time a "teddy bear cactus" (jumping cholla) stuck my legs together and I thought I'd been bitten by a rattlesnake. There was an emergency sixteen-mile trek out of the Glacier Peak Wilderness, and the time I was treed by a bear eight miles from camp, not to mention a terrifying but hilarious experience involving a mountain lion, a bear, and a pack of coyotes in a deep, dark canyon in the Santa Teresa Mountains.

## BY MY SIDE

It was during these years that I met and married Karey. I first saw her while I was helping lead a high school ministry at a church in Tucson. I was then a geology graduate student at the University of Arizona and she was only in high school, so I assumed I was too old for her. Also I figured I was just too square.

Years later we got to know each other better. One summer when one of my brothers came to Tucson with a friend, Karey came along with us every weekend as we headed for the Graham Mountains to escape the Arizona heat. Her mother was overjoyed because we were clean-cut (i.e., old-fashioned) Christian guys. One of our favorite pastimes was to cruise desert roads at night after heavy rains, hunting tarantulas and rattlesnakes. We kept the tarantulas in our house to control the cockroaches. The rattlesnakes we roasted over campfires and ate with fresh corn and artichokes. Karey thought it was a real kick.

> My parents knew what was calling me.

When Karey and I were together at her home, she played the piano and I sang. We discussed theology for hours, ministered together through several musical dramas, shared cross-country ski trips, and backpacked all over Arizona. After a year or so Karey had become my best friend, and I realized this was what I'd missed in all my past relationships with girls: friendship.

In November of 1975, Karey and I eloped (with the consent of all four parents), just as my own parents had done nearly thirty years earlier. We were married atop Mount Graham, an alpine island in the desert of Arizona overlooking my thesis area, Stockton Pass. The ceremony took place in a semicircle of aspen trees at the edge of a meadow. To the east, over the pastor's shoulder, a crescent moon was visible, and a cool desert wind was blowing in our faces. We have only one wedding photo, taken by the pastor—a silhouette of the bride and groom against a gold and crimson setting sun.

We honeymooned in a backpacking tent, which I figured would be good preparation for a geological prospecting trip on the horizon. My company was planning to send us to Halls Creek in Australia's northwestern desert to search for massive sulfide copper and gold deposits. We would be dry camping hundreds of miles from the nearest town, among world-renowned desert death adders whose bites—I'd heard—can kill a human in a matter of seconds. But the Australia trip never happened; the price of copper plunged and the company abandoned metal exploration in that part of the world.

Instead I continued geological research in Arizona with Karey by my side. Some experiences were more hair-raising than others. Not long after we learned Karey was pregnant with our first child, we were guided on horseback to a copper prospect near Zane Grey's cabin in the Mogollon Rim country of Arizona. Our hosts provided Karey a horse but failed to tighten the cinch. On the trail the saddle slipped, and all of a sudden my bride was hanging upside down under the horse! That night we were treated to a steak dinner, cooked over an open fire, accompanied by coffee made in an antediluvian pot with water scooped from a stagnant pool filled with fermenting oak leaves. I can still taste it—full-bodied, with a slight hint of oxidation and a tinge of tannic acid. Later we reclined in an old prospector's cabin on rusty bedsprings that had once been the insides of a mattress, and which the resident mice used as a jungle gym all night long.

## A FAMILY TOGETHER

Even after our children were born, Karey continued traveling with me through the great outdoors that was my workplace. Most geologists' wives soon grow tired of living in cabins and tents without telephones, television, running water, or toilet seats. But Karey marched to a different drummer, and she spent the late 1970s roaming the backcountry of the American West with two small children and one big one. She was satisfied to set up housekeeping wherever we were—in a cabin, motel, tent, or the back of our four-wheel-drive vehicle.

Why? Because she was determined to keep our family together. While I totally agreed with her motivation, taking everybody along on every trip was a colossal logistical challenge. I look back now and wonder why I didn't buy a

> *Karey was determined to keep our family together.*

trailer. Instead, I filled our 4x4 Chevy Blazer to the gills every trip with playpens, diaper pails, baby food, cribs, suitcases, toys, typewriter, sewing machine, and guitar. The packing process, which I did for more than ten years, never ceased to be a giant jigsaw puzzle challenge.

Was it worth the effort? Absolutely. We would do it again in a heartbeat.

Since Karey didn't have the luxuries and entertainments

her peers were enjoying, she read books purchased primarily at used bookstores in out-of-the-way places we visited. In no time books began to accumulate in the vehicle, in cabins, in tents, wherever we went. This further complicated my packing job, but it was well worth it because, as we traveled, we often discussed her latest reading.

I was only mildly infected with the used book bug until one fateful day when we attended an open-air auction in southern Wisconsin. We were just spectators enjoying the auction until a box of old books came up. When no one bid on them, we bought them all for seventy-five cents. Then we read them—all—and in the process became addicted to books, particularly old hardbacks and classics.

When some people travel they can't pass an antique shop. For us, used bookstores whispered our names so tantalizingly we simply had to stop. Once, I wanted Karey to experience an authentic Finnish sauna in Michigan's Upper Peninsula. In the cedar-scented lobby of the building that housed the sauna, old books were for sale—hundreds of them rescued when a nearby one-room schoolhouse shut its doors. We were drawn like mice to cheese, like moths to the lantern, like trout to a worm...you get the point. I can't even remember if we made it to the sauna. But I do remember the books.

My bent toward research, combined with Karey's passion for reading—which she soon passed along to me—became a lifelong search for knowledge and truth through the written word. It's a little like searching for gold. And once we find a nugget of truth, it's very hard for us to part with the source. Maybe that's one reason we have over six thousand volumes nestled here and there in our home.

## A SEARCH FOR THE MYSTERY

With our desire to continue a traveling lifestyle, by the time our children reached school age we had decided to home-school—actually, "road-school." Integrating this with the parenting approach I'd inherited from my parents made for an interesting combination.

At times we were challenged by our friends and relatives about our unique lifestyle. As we formulated and verbalized our philosophy of parenting in response, we began to receive invitations to speak and write on the subject, and I wrote a number of songs on this theme. Our immersion in "process" fueled

> *It was clear that my parents knew something very few parenting books touched on.*

our passion to be the best parents we could be and to help others do the same. Karey and I were motivated to read all the latest parenting books we could find.

Soon thousands of people encouraged us, challenged us, and shared their insights into parenting. We discovered that many parents were anxious to learn from us, but we struggled for just the right words to communicate with precision what we knew in our hearts.

As we did, it became increasingly clear to us that my parents knew something very few books touched on. So we went to visit them.

We peppered Mom and Dad with questions, trying to find the elusive, mysterious ingredient that had made their parenting such a success.

"Did you ever go out on weekly dates like most modern

marriage manuals recommend?" I asked.

"We did everything together as a family," they replied. "We wouldn't think of going off without our boys."

So much for "date night."

"Did you treat each of us differently, or all the same?"

"We always tried to treat you the same, while also trying to find what special talent each of you had. We believe that respect for each family member, no matter their age, is extremely important."

The conversation went on for some time, but the magical ingredient didn't make itself known to Karey and me that day. My parents were intrigued by the intensity of our search for their silver bullet, and nearly as mystified. As far as they were concerned, they'd just done what came naturally—what had seemed right to them at the time.

Karey and I decided my parents' integrated lifestyle defined them so completely that it was impossible to identify any single magic ingredient. Clearly they had practiced many of the things we found in the parenting books. In fact, much of what they had done would become "leading edge" a generation later. But still the key to their success eluded us.


## FINDING THE WORDS

By the spring of 1996, Karey and I had accumulated thousands of books—plus one filing cabinet full of notes and articles— without a clear answer. But on Easter Sunday our pastor entitled his message "Romancing the Stones." He was thinking of the Pharisees and the hardness of their hearts toward the love and grace of God, especially as expressed through Jesus.

As I listened, something happened in the part of my brain that was perpetually pondering the parenting puzzle. The words romance and child suddenly came together...and they've stayed together ever since.

Interestingly, Karey had already put these words together a few months earlier, but somehow I hadn't recognized their significance. In *Hearth and Home* she'd written about filling our daily life "with God's love and words" so that we lead our children's hearts heavenward. "Like a courtship," she wrote, "we are romancing their hearts."[3]

For several months we tried out the phrase "romancing your child's heart" on anyone who would listen. Almost everyone knew immediately what we meant—not another set of principles or a list of rules, but an invitation to a new way of thinking about parenting. Even more, it was a new way of thinking about living. This was the magic ingredient we'd been trying so hard to identify all those years.

Plenty of books out there offer recipes for cookie-cutter parenting. One reason Karey and I missed the point for so long was that we devoured these books ad nauseam, and they led us into the wrong realm—the realm of doing.

Effective parenting is partly about doing, and it starts even before the children are born. We talk about them, discussing how many we want and how we'll raise them. We dream dreams, buy books, and pray prayers. We design our houses, select our vehicles, and even choose our careers with our children in mind.

After their birth we spend thousands of dollars and thousands of hours educating and mentoring them. We buy swing sets, build tree houses, and order truckloads of sand. We provide musical instruments, computers, and sports equipment. We drive them to countless music lessons and athletic events.

But what remains when they finally leave home one day? Are we left with garages full of tennis shoes, old blue jeans, car seats, rocks, broken toys, and baseball gloves? Or have we built relationships, deep and strong, that will only get better over time?

We can do, do, and do until the cows come home and still end up estranged from our children. The missing element in so many parent-child relationships is not a matter of doing—but being.

## Two Treasure Hunters

Am I talking never-never land here? Not at all.

Let's go back to Wisconsin for a moment—to another time, another little boy, and another grandfather romancing that little boy's heart.

The two of them are on a mission through the grandfather's Christmas tree farm. Their joint goal is to select two Christmas trees, one for the boy's parents and one for his grandparents. In the dim silver sunlight of that December day, the treasure hunters meander through the lacy, fragrant boughs, examining countless trees—lingering at one, circling another.

> Sometimes people laugh and say the family I describe couldn't possibly exist.

As they wander, someone else follows at a distance, close enough to hear their dialogue yet far enough away he might as well be invisible. It's the boy's father. He hears the man and boy judging and appraising each tree as if they're making the decision of a lifetime.

They are, but it's not about trees.

From their conversation, several things are apparent. There's no other place the grandfather would rather be. He's in no hurry, and he lets the child lead as they walk from tree to tree. He never forces or presses for a decision. Occasionally he does suggest a tree, but it's clear he has no agenda. He patiently awaits the boy's verdict, weighing it with all seriousness and respect, though the ten-year-old has little experience in such matters.

When the boy suggests one that's too tall, the grandfather doesn't focus on the waste. "If we cut off the lower two feet," he says, "it would be a great tree for you, and you could make wreaths from the extra boughs."

When they reach an impasse, the grandfather suggests they jump on his four-wheeler, which he has taught the boy to drive. Off they go to a remote part of the farm. After several hours, they've each cut a tree.

Later the boy spends an entire day intently decorating the tree that was a special gift from his grandfather. The family is unanimous—there has never been a more beautiful Christmas tree than this one.

The boy in this story isn't me. He's my son. And the grandpa is my father. As I witnessed their Christmas tree hunt not long ago, I was reminded of the unusual family to which I belong. Surely such moments of romance are rare. Seeing the two of them together brought back memories of my own childhood.

Sometimes, before I tell people this story is real, they laugh and say the family I describe couldn't possibly exist. The real world doesn't produce whole families where peace, respect, trust, and unconditional love reign supreme. Children always rebel at some point; it's naive to think they could be their parents' best friends and willingly obey them.

Really?

## GIVING THE FINEST PART

In the summer of 2000, Karey and I spoke at a weeklong conference at Sandy Cove on Chesapeake Bay. The message of "Romancing Your Child's Heart" touched one of the fathers in a special way. Toward the end of the week he shared his story with us.

"Until this week," Steve said, "I've misunderstood my father—never really appreciating him. He wasn't the kind of father who would play ball with me and do all those things the parenting books say a father should do. So I thought he'd somehow failed me."

Tears began to flow as Steve continued: "But my father did pour his music into my life—it was all he knew. I never realized until now that when my father shared his first love—his passion—with me, he was romancing me to God the only way he knew how. He included me—trained me and taught me his music—and now he's so proud of my music. He was successful as a father because he won my heart for God by giving the finest part of himself to me."

Steve concluded, "I see it clearly now—the idea of the

Larger Story—the Romance—and I intend to do this for my children, to romance their hearts to God. I thought I was on track, focusing primarily on teaching them biblical truth and training them in proper behavior, but I was missing the true prize. I'm going to enter the contest for their hearts."

Steve wrote a song that week and sang it for the conference participants. Here are a few lines:

*Plans of the heart are made by man.*
*The Lord our God has given such to me.*
*Open my eyes, allowing me to see*
*The tender hearts You placed within my hand.*
*I can hear them screaming for romance.*

*Chorus:*
*Fairy tales are more than fantasy.*
*I believe that they come true within a child's heart.*
*Their hearts can be both ravished and romanced.*
*Before mine are old I'm gonna take the chance,*
*And fill their hearts with fairy-tale romance.*[4]

## EVERYONE HAS A STORY

This concept of romancing a child's heart has the potential to radically transform our lives as parents as we give our children something to someday write, speak, or sing about.

Everyone has a story. Or rather, everyone is living a story, and that story is part of a Larger Story, the one God has been telling since forever. It's His Story, found in the pages of the

Bible, a romance describing how deeply, extravagantly, and sacrificially God loves us, pursues us, and woos us to Himself.

God chose to use story as a means of explaining who He is and what He desires of us. And Jesus often used story—in the form of parables—to speak of God, to reveal the deeper truths of His love and grace, to show us how to have a living relationship with Him by faith.

Our Christian faith is less about doing than being—specifically, being in a relationship. And this personal relationship must precede anything we try to do, or else the romance we offer our children will be little more than pretense.

# Chapter 3

# Living the Larger Story

*If you knew you had one year*
*Left to live, left to love,*
*Would you live to love?*
*What would you do*
*If you knew?*

O ften it takes a crisis to help parents see the Larger Story more clearly.

When our son Travis was three years old, he had a bout with viral meningitis. He was in constant pain and couldn't walk. He had a fever of 103 degrees for three weeks, then developed an arthritic condition the doctors couldn't diagnose. We visited numerous physicians for test after test.

One of the most difficult was the spinal tap. We had to hold little Travis still while the doctor stuck a long needle between the vertebrae of his back. I'll never forget how, when the fluid came out clear, the doctor said, "Praise the Lord. It's not bacterial." However, no one could explain what was causing our son's joints to swell.

The only thing that seemed to soothe Travis was the

Dallas Holm song "I Saw the Lord." I played it over and over for him.

Meanwhile, I was in a desperate state. Will he survive? Will he be disabled? Will he be able to make it in life? The questions went on forever. I was paralyzed by the scenarios that kept running through my analytical mind.

Finally, I hit a point of emotional exhaustion. All I could do was literally cast myself on my face before God under a pine tree behind our house. I gave up hope from any human perspective and surrendered to Him. At that moment I found peace in the knowledge that I could trust Him with our son's life.

In that encounter, I touched eternity. It was the true moment of relief for me—even more than the moment several weeks later when we found out from a team of specialists that the arthritis was only a reactionary form caused by the virus leaving Travis's body; it would burn itself out within a few weeks with no lasting effects.

Karey processed the whole situation differently. While I had brooded over the if-onlys of the past and the what-ifs of the future, Karey stayed focused on the present as she calmly cared for Travis, hour after hour, day after day. Throughout this experience she felt a comforting sense of serenity—the peace that passes all understanding—and was able to guard her heart and mind.

> *In the Larger Story which includes our smaller stories we live happily ever after.*

I had viewed Travis's crisis from a temporal perspective; Karey saw it through eyes of faith. She could live with the tension of not knowing how this particular chapter of Travis's story would end because she knew that in the Larger Story—which includes our smaller stories, but never ends—all of us would live happily ever after.

## AFTER THE SHADOWS

C. S. Lewis was fond of speaking of this natural world as the shadowlands, where the shadows of the supernatural fall. While the shadows themselves seem real, our challenge is to trace back the shadows—even the shadow of death—to the realities behind them, the eternal realities of the Larger Story.

Do you remember the final paragraph in the final book of Lewis's Chronicles of Narnia?

> And for us this is the end of all the stories, and we can most truly say that they all lived happily ever after. But for them it was only the beginning of the real story. All their life in this world and all their adventures in Narnia had only been the cover and the title page: now at last they were beginning Chapter One of the Great Story, which no one on earth has read: which goes on forever: in which every chapter is better than the one before.[5]

The pure drama and deep truth of these few words are never lost on children. The Larger Story is burned into their hearts, where it retains the ability to illuminate even their dark times with the light of eternal truth.

One of my friends remembers being overwhelmed with

emotion as he read this passage to his son, who at that moment was lingering between life and death while battling a mysterious disease that had already killed his younger brother. The father's emotion came from the contrast between the deep truth the story expressed and his deep longing that this son would not be taken from him as another had been. He was reminded that even in the valley of the shadow of death, neither he nor his son need fear any evil. The Larger Story guaranteed that God was with them, and always would be. (The boy lived, by the way.)

## A STORY AND A STORYTELLER

All human beings know intuitively that there's a Larger Story. Paul counted on this while speaking with the men of Athens, mentioning their altar "to the unknown god" as a bridge to the true and knowable God "who made the world and everything in it" and who is "Lord of heaven and earth." This God set in motion the story's script: He "made from one blood every nation of men," Paul said, then He "determined their preappointed times and the boundaries of their dwellings," all for a purpose: The preconceived plot keeps advancing as people "seek the Lord," as they "grope for Him and find Him, though He is not far from each one of us; for in Him we live and move and have our being" (Acts 17:22–28). By the Author's design, the Story inherently draws seekers to Himself.

This is why G. K. Chesterton could say (in *Orthodoxy: The Romance of Faith*), "I had always felt life first as a story; and if there is a story there is a storyteller."[6]

No wonder we're all "desperate for something larger to give our lives transcendence," as Brent Curtis and John Eldredge remind us in *The Sacred Romance;* yet many of us "live our lives like a movie we've arrived at twenty minutes late. The action is well underway and we haven't a clue what's happening.... Worse, we try to interpret the meaning of life with only fragments, isolated incidents, feelings, and images without reference to the story of which these scenes are merely a part."[7]

In such clueless living we reflect nothing better than the prevailing non-Christian worldview that tends toward morbidity, skepticism, pragmatism, even moral anarchy. Nothing hangs together, and there's no context. We find it nearly impossible to see the big picture.

Some "Story-less" people go to a movie like Titanic six or seven times, looking for their script. Woven through the special effects, the historical narrative, the cultural clashes, and the fornication, there is Story—a tale of the kind of bravery and sacrifice that are a picture of Christ's sacrificial love on Calvary. Hollywood can't seem to keep this gospel out of its stories. Like the pagan philosophers of Athens, they're desperately building altars to an unknown god.

Only the Christian worldview can adequately clarify the Larger Story. I'm in relationship with God, my Creator—the author of the oldest Story in the world, yet a Story that's forever young, written by Someone whose heart is unceasingly good. The flow of history and of the ages is a passionate drama that includes a cosmic conflict between God and Satan, good and evil—what the Greeks would call an epic. But it's also a love story, rendered more powerful by the backdrop of spiritual warfare. Just as God could crush Satan at any time, He could also force humans to "love" and serve Him. Instead, He came to earth in person to romance and rescue His bride, in a story more magically romantic than any ever told.

## ONLY HERE AND NOW

We can enter and participate in this Story only in the present, the here and now—because Story is lived only in the present. Our human nature is distracted by the hustle and bustle, the responsibilities, and the self-imposed goals that fill our lives, so that often we become too occupied with what has happened or may happen to focus on what is actually happening. These distractions prevent us from living in the Larger Story and being conscious of God's script.

> *The Story is forever young, written by Someone whose heart is unceasingly good.*

Such distraction is exactly Satan's design, according to what C. S. Lewis's Screwtape writes to the junior devil Wormwood:

The humans live in time, but our Enemy [God] destines them to eternity. He therefore, I believe, wants them to attend chiefly to two things, to eternity itself and to that point of time which they call the Present. For the present is that point at which time touches eternity. Of the present moment, and of it only, humans have an experience analogous to the experience which our Enemy has of reality as a whole; in it alone freedom and actuality are offered them. He would therefore have them continually concerned either with eternity (which means being concerned with Him) or with the Present—either meditating on their eternal union with, or separation from Himself, or else obeying the present voice of conscience, bearing the present cross, receiving the present grace, giving thanks for the present pleasure.... Our business is to get them away from the eternal and from the Present.... We want a whole race perpetually in pursuit of the rainbow's end, never honest, nor kind, nor happy now, but always using as mere fuel wherewith to heap the altar of the Future every real gift which is offered them in the Present.[8]

## GLADNESS FOR EVERYTHING

What will happen for our children if we as parents live in the Larger Story, if we touch eternity in the present and follow the script God has written for us?

Our children will witness an eternal drama directed by God. The beauty in our lives will dazzle our children—and woo them. They'll see eternity in the way we invest our resources, talents, and time, and this will provide them a transcendent purpose and an ultimate framework for understanding all of reality.

As they see us bowing before God and serving others, tremors will pass down our children's spines because they'll begin to suspect God really is real. The intimate presence of the Holy Spirit, unleashing the power of a personal God in our lives, will allow them to witness awe-inspiring encounters. They'll see how relationship is central in all we do. They'll experience the passionate love God has for them and be irresistibly drawn to Him as they respond to the Romance.

Our children will realize they're made for a larger drama, and they'll greet each new day with wonder and joy as each new page of the Romance is turned.

Hearing me say such things, some people see me as a hopeless optimist. They call me Pollyanna, which is okay because I've read the book Pollyanna. It's a marvelous tale of how a little orphan girl, with every right to be bitter, transforms an entire New England town by teaching the "glad game" she learned from her minister father before he died. The glad game turns the shadowland on its head by finding a way to be glad for whatever happens.

> *God has written a one-of-a-kind script for each of us to follow.*

One of the main characters, Dr. Chilton, describes Pollyanna's remarkable effect on many of his patients, which he says is "better than a six-quart bottle of tonic."

His nurse says, "Indeed! And what are the special ingredients of this wonderworking tonic of hers?"

"As near as I can find out," replies the doctor, "it is an overwhelming, unquenchable gladness for everything that has happened or is going to happen."[9]

The reason so many critics attack a Pollyanna perspective is that childlike faith is a powerful threat to the sophisticated spirit of our age. It's often culturally incorrect to speak of such powerful realities as truth, joy, purpose, and meaning. Yet these things, straight from the heart of God, are what the Story is all about.

## THE WAY OF WISDOM

As we grow in our own conscious awareness of this Larger Story, how can we practically help our children do the same? It's something far different from teaching the Scriptures as a manual of morality to absorb and memorize.

Proverbs tells us that our heavenly Father has created a treasure hunt for each of us. We're told to search for the hidden treasure of wisdom, a treasure of incomparable value. The way of wisdom is not only a story, but a specific kind of story— one about a quest for treasure. The drama of this search is what beautifies our life and romances our children to God.

I believe the way of wisdom described in Proverbs is the literal and spiritual path that almighty God has designed for each of us to walk through this life. The path is always unique; God has written a one-of-a-kind script for each of us to follow. We shouldn't be envious or judgmental of other people's stories because we all have our own, as do our children. For some, there may be moments of high risk; for others, the endurance of daily discipline, or the gift of suffering, or the burden of leadership, or perhaps overcoming the challenges and dangers of wealth.

I also believe that the ability and passion to live in this way of wisdom are best taught to children through stories. Stories bring to life biblical knowledge, doctrine, character, and virtue—they show us how to apply these to life according to God's will.

Children who grow up hearing and seeing stories are far better prepared for true living. Stories give them the closest thing to behind-the-wheel driving practice.

However—and this is crucial—we as parents need to select carefully the stories to which our children are exposed. Our challenge is to find stories through which the Larger Story runs like a thread. Besides the biblical narratives, these can also include classics, great books and films, stories we create as we go, and family traditions.

## REHEARSAL FOR LIFE

Children by their very nature live in their imaginations—in stories. Their worlds are large, filled with wonder, adventure, and drama. Wisely chosen stories take advantage of this and prepare them to participate wisely in the pageant called life. They learn the props and set, and become experienced in improvising on the story line through their moral imagination.

For children raised this way, their whole childhood and adolescence is a rehearsal for living as adults. They're practiced in the art of living in the Larger Story scripted and choreographed by God. They don't need to search for meaning—they've found it already. They're preoccupied, enthralled, fascinated, captivated by the Larger Story, like deer panting after the water—people after God's own heart.

They've learned to see their own story as an adventure. John Eldredge, in *Wild at Heart,* speaks of adventure as "a deeply spiritual longing written into the soul of man. It's not just about having 'fun.' Adventure requires something of us, puts us to the test."[10] I believe he's referring to the way of wisdom.

It's a path to follow with bated breath and trembling excitement. We look at the world with wide-eyed wonder and awe, and we understand the implications of the central truth of the Larger Story—that in Him we live, and in Him we move, and in Him we have our being.

# Chapter 4

# The Dynamics
# of Story

*Her work seems never to end,*
*And lately her days run together,*
*But she knows the page she'll write tonight*
*Will last forever.*

"The Best Days"

One Christmas Eve when I was very young, my aunt and uncle gave me a beautiful hardback book, *Marian's Big Book of Bible Stories.*[11] The author, Marian Schoolland, ended her preface with this sentence: "If this book leads some little heart and mind to know and love God it will not have been written in vain." She knew the power stories exert upon a child.

So did my aunt. Inside the cover, she had written me these words: "Tell Mommy to read you a story every day."

For years my mother read to me from this book. As she turned the pages, I studied and savored the wonderfully colored pictures and listened as she read over and over my favorite chapters: how the world began, and how God made people; the story of the Flood, and of Jericho's falling walls; the deeds of Samson, of David, of Elijah; how Jesus walked on water, and how He went up to heaven.

God's primary way of communicating His character, His love, and His will has always been through stories—the only vehicle capable of carrying a significant cargo of truth to the human heart as He Himself designed it.

> *Stories carry the message, not just the information.*

Truth is conveyed to our hearts most powerfully in stories because stories carry the message, not just the information. That's why so many books of the Bible are pure narratives, each revealing something special about God and His way with us. Think of Job, Hosea, Daniel, Joshua, Ruth, Esther, and many more. Whole sections of the Bible are stories—from the history of Israel to the Gospels, where we see and hear Jesus, the best storyteller of all.

Delivering His message largely through stories, Jesus used parables to communicate divine truth directly to the human heart by starting with what His hearers knew—a barren fig tree, a fine pearl, a great banquet, hidden treasure—then nudging them toward what, or more accurately, whom He wanted them to know better. Those whose hearts were open to His message understood and believed.

By contrast, the religious leaders of Jesus' day, with their onerous rules and regulations, often did not or could not understand His meaning because of their preconceptions, prejudice, and hardness of heart. They lived in a different paradigm, and they preferred to remain there. Sometimes, of course, they realized He was describing them, which fueled their anger and desire to be rid of Him. Imagine being confident in your righteousness, only to hear

Jesus publicly compare you to a whitewashed tomb full of rotting flesh.

## DAZZLED BY GOD'S TRUTH

My perception is that the greater part of the Christian church today—including many Christian parents—are accustomed to thinking of faith in cognitive, intellectual terms, of rules and regulations that so easily produce the same dead orthodoxy, legalism, pride, and self-righteousness that the Pharisees exhibited. They focus on teaching their children God's Bible and doctrines, while the God who inspired the Bible wants to win their children's hearts—which surely is related not so much to knowing about Him as to knowing Him, personally.

Since I became a Christian, I've probably sat through more than two thousand sermons—most of them preached in three-point Greek logic, imparting information I can't recall. I regretfully admit that on occasion I've nearly dozed off prior to the preacher's final point. My wake-up call came when I realized my entire family was having the same problem. Surely I didn't want my children inoculated against faith. I wanted them inspired to discover faith's meaning in their own lives.

These days, however, I often find myself wishing in church that the message would never end, a sentiment shared by my family. As we drive home we animatedly discuss the truth the message carried. I'm confident that if I bring unbelieving friends to the service they'll be dazzled by God's truth.

The difference: Our pastor preaches in "story." I'm not speaking of a few illustrations, stories, or jokes designed to keep the audience awake. He's not an entertainer. He's a story-teller. He often teaches in a "story hermeneutic"—crafting his entire message around a story. The powerful truth carried to our hearts each Sunday on the vehicle of story breaks spiritual dams, flooding our lives with the inspiring, motivating, and convicting meaning of the "living and active" Word of God, that "judges the thoughts and attitudes of the heart" (Hebrews 4:12, NIV).

Stories sneak past the screens and filters of our rational minds. Instead of stowing bare facts in the files of our intellect, stories infect our spirit, touching and moving our inner being. A well-told story can sweep through the heart, rearranging the meaning of facts and ideas lodged in our mind as we react to the drama, the suspense, the anticipated outcome.

That's why children learn almost nothing from abstraction-laden instruction, and almost everything from stories. Abstractions are impersonal and detached; stories are practical and personal.

Children learn through stories because they internalize them—they become the characters. When a character fails, lessons are learned that will provide guidance when the child faces adult ambiguities. When good triumphs over evil, a seed is planted that will someday grow into faith that God is good and can be trusted. When the characters live happily ever after, the child is connected, if only for an instant, with the Larger Story of which fairy tales are but a mere reflection—the Story that promises eternal happiness for those who come to God by faith.

## STEALING PAST THE DRAGONS

We can tell our children what to do, or how to do something. We can teach them morals and rules. But what we say in that regard is likely to go in one ear and out the other unless we give them handles by which to grab the meanings we wish to communicate.

Good stories carry the freight of truth without moralizing. The best stories show us God's reality, developing within us a thirst to experience it, not just know about it.

In *On Stories,* C. S. Lewis recalls "a certain inhibition, which had paralyzed much of my own religion in childhood."

Why did one find it so hard to feel as one was told one ought to feel about God or about the sufferings of Christ? I thought the chief reason was that one was told one ought to. An obligation to feel can freeze feelings. And reverence itself did harm. The whole subject was associated with lowered voices; almost as if it were something medical.

Lewis asked himself,

But supposing that by casting all these things into an imaginary world, stripping them of their stained-glass and Sunday School associations, one could make them for the first time appear in their real potency? Could one not thus steal past those watchful dragons? I thought one could.[12]

Chuck Bolte, who was executive producer of the popular *Odyssey* radio stories, told me his mission was to produce good stories that in themselves carried God's truth to the listener by way of the "theater of the mind." He had a strong faith in the power of story as a ministry tool and believed that stories built around sermonettes do not reach the heart. Instead he operated on this premise: "Truth emanates out of story, and not the reverse." He and his colleagues used stories to "steal past the dragons," allowing children to hear the truth, not because someone said they ought to listen but because they wanted to.

## THE ROLE OF STORY IN OUR MEMORIES

When God wants us to remember something, He uses a story instead of a list of principles or rules. Even the Ten Commandments appear in the middle of a long story, and Matthew's account of Jesus' Golden Rule, which summarizes the meaning of the Law and the Prophets, occurs in the context of a series of parables.

My friend, author Joe Wheeler, describes how stories "dig into conscious memory and then keep digging until they reach our subconscious memory," where they become "part of us, part of our motivations, part of all that we think and say and do."[13]

In their book *Storytelling*, Norma Livo and Sandra Rietz tell us that we remember events better when we shape our memories into stories—even though that shaping in itself may change the memory. And our "storied events" are "bigger" than the events themselves, because "they have been invested with the greater truth of 'story.'"[14]

Isn't it possible God built the process of storying into human memory as the primary organizer of information and ideas? If so, we aren't empty vessels into which perceptions passively pour; we have a built-in "operating system" through which we actively organize and structure our experiences. This story-based system gives us the ability to think in context—and ultimately, the ability to experience God's truth.

## SUPPORT FROM SCIENCE

Recent scientific studies provide insight into why God has chosen to reveal Himself and His will for us primarily through stories. Dr. Renée Fuller, a professor of physiological psychology, theorized from her work with mentally retarded students that ministories are the basic cognitive units of human learning—the deep structure of language. Dr. Fuller calls these units "story engrams," from the word used to describe the change in neural tissue

> *Our story-based "operating system" gives us the ability to experience God's truth.*

that produces persistence of memory. They comprise a thing (noun) that acts or is acted upon (verb), and are the building blocks of human understanding. So both an infant's first word—a noun with a verb implied—and the most convoluted novel share something in common: Both tell a story.

The patterning of ideas is what gives a story its power to communicate truth. Simple truth is communicated when the arrangement is linear: $A + B = C$. Most traditional education, whether it occurs in grammar school, Sunday school, or medical school, expects its students to memorize facts arranged in this pattern, or in no pattern at all. However, the most profound truth—that is, truth that affects our hearts while achieving a change in our memories (an engram)—is usually conveyed in a story where the ideas are arranged in nonlinear logic.

Well-crafted stories capture our attention, ambush our hearts, then dazzle us with beauty and resolution. They're more than just a series of logical ideas or a grammatically correct arrangement of words. In fact, sometimes stories don't involve words at all.

One of my colleagues—an agnostic—wept when he first saw Michelangelo's David. At that moment his soul and the soul of the artist met, transcending time and connecting my colleague with the eternal creative Spirit of God in the story this sculpture portrays.

Or recall with me Rembrandt's painting of Christ's descent from the cross, in which the artist placed himself, mourning, at the foot of the cross as one of those helping to remove Christ's body. Without words, Rembrandt made a powerful statement about the state of his own heart—and a subtle statement about what the state of viewers' hearts should be. Were the artist standing in a corner of the painting, his back mostly turned to the cross, we would come away with an entirely different impression. Without doubt, this particular masterpiece—indeed every true masterpiece, whether a novel, movie, opera, painting, photograph, poem, play, sculpture, symphony, or song—tells a story.

By contrast, modern art is notorious for not telling a story, other than the "story" that there is no story. The fragmented, sometimes chaotic nature of this type of art presents the idea of a Story-less universe. In the same way, music without a coherent melody or chord resolution is Story-less. These trends, among many others, reflect the basic secular mindset of our times: We're here as a result of chance, and life is going nowhere and is fundamentally without meaning. Not only does this type of art have no meaning, but no one cares that it doesn't.

## FAIRY TALES AND FANTASIES

Stories teach to the heart—but for parents, certain kinds of stories are better structured to do this for their children than others.

Perhaps to some modern Christian parents, fairy tales and fantasies may not seem relevant or beneficial because the stories aren't "real." But this kind of story connects us with the most real things of all—a realm beyond our senses—the supernatural realm of God. Scientific realism (data and logic) is not enough. Our word fantasy comes from the Greek for "a making visible."[15]

Fantasies make visible the invisible. Fairy tales open the door to the supernatural, tapping a universal longing in the heart of every child and adult to connect with eternity.

A traditional fairy tale involves clearly defined characters engaged in a conflict between good and evil. The story has a beginning, follows a linear arrow of time, and has an end. Good ultimately triumphs, and the characters live happily ever after. This pattern is "Christian," in contrast with the modern story that often follows a circular, relativistic path leading to nonresolution.

Children need fairy tales as a part of their moral training, for this type of story mirrors the Larger Story. It impresses that pattern in their minds as they participate in their imaginations. This is important practical training for the challenges they'll face as adults.

We adults need fairy tales, too, to keep alive the trusting child still within us—the part that allows us, according to Jesus, to enter into the kingdom of heaven. And according to C. S. Lewis, the best test of a good children's story is whether adults as well as children enjoy it.[16]

> *We need fairy tales to keep alive the trusting child still within us.*

Fairy tales stimulate what has been called a child's "moral imagination." A moral imagination enables people to think for themselves, to differentiate right from wrong, to discern what is truly good and righteous in the complex adult world where simple learned rules don't suffice because we can't anticipate every situation.

Even the gospel is a fairy tale in the highest sense, the kind of story our world requires, as Frederick Buechner explains in *Telling the Truth: The Gospel as Tragedy, Comedy and Fairy Tale:*

It is a world of magic and mystery, of deep darkness and flickering starlight. It is a world where terrible things happen and wonderful things too. It is a world where goodness is pitted against evil, love against hate, order against chaos, in a great struggle.... Yet for all its confusion and wildness, it is a world where the battle goes ultimately to the good, who live happily ever after, and where in the long run, everybody, good and evil alike, becomes known by his true name.... That is the fairy tale of the Gospel with, of course, one critical difference from all other fairy tales, which is that the claim made for it is that it is true, that it not only happened once upon a time, but has kept on happening ever since and is happening still.[17]

## OUR CHILDREN'S MORAL IMAGINATIONS

In *Tending the Heart of Virtue,* theologian Vigen Guroian explores the moral and religious value of fairy tales and other fantasy stories written for children. His goal is to "demonstrate how fairy tales feed the moral imagination with the best food."[18]

His book serves as a wise and understanding guide for parents interested in teaching character and virtues with stories. He would say, however, that before you try to use such stories to teach others you must experience them yourself—become as a child and let the stories touch and move your heart.

Guroian looks at how life-impacting lessons permeate such stories as *Pinocchio, The Velveteen Rabbit, The Little Mermaid, The Wind in the Willows, Charlotte's Web, Bambi, The Snow Queen, The Princess and the Goblin, Prince Caspian,* and *The Lion, the Witch and the Wardrobe.* The original, unabridged versions of these stories are vastly different from their modern diluted and perverted video counterparts. They were written from a Christian worldview and are filled with gospel imagery and themes.

The issues the author finds (or made me think of) in these stories include these:

- Life and death
- Joy and sorrow
- Failure and resilience
- A sense of mission and meaning
- The natural and supernatural—visible and invisible
- Temptation, sin, forgiveness, and reconciliation
- Betrayal and loyalty
- Pain and pleasure
- Pride, prejudice, greed, envy, fear
- Romance, truth, beauty, and freedom

Guroian identifies positive influences in these stories that help develop character traits like courage, compassion, humility, kindness, self-control, generosity, patience, persistence, willingness to sacrifice, dependability, truthfulness, and responsibility.

In addition to the children's stories he discusses, he lists others worth absorbing, such as *The Ugly Duckling, Where the Wild Things Are, Snow White and the Seven Dwarfs, The Reluctant Dragon, The Trumpet and the Swan,* and *The King and the Golden River.*

He also mentions a telling incident about his son, Rafi, when he was asked in a college application to name the books from his childhood that meant the most to him. Rafi replied that C. S. Lewis's Narnia chronicles were the most memorable because they left him "with standards to live by"[19]—evidence again that children learn values not from our moralizing or sermonizing, but from our stories.

## THE FAVORITES

But my favorite stories are those that haven't been written down. They've been told or sung around the campfire, on front porches, during a walk through the woods, or around the dinner table. Such stories were completely original, revealing the narrator's soul, which then connected with mine.

My kids share the same perspective. While Karey and I probably told or read a thousand tales to our kids as they grew up, what they remember most vividly are the stories arising from conversations around the table or with guests. The truths learned there were carried to their hearts.

After writing a final exam in a political science course at college, Travis was approached by the professor who asked him, in a tone that implied he must have cheated or plagiarized, where he'd gotten such ideas.

"From discussions around the family dining room table as I grew up," Travis replied.

## A START IN STORY-TELLING

How do we as parents learn to tell stories? Here are some ideas:

- Invite interesting people for dinner and ask them questions (and let your children ask, too).
- Read some of the children's stories mentioned in this chapter.
- Listen to audio tapes with your children, like the *Odyssey* radio series from Focus on the Family.

- · Read aloud biographies of great people, or historical fiction.
- · Watch and discuss quality videos and great films.
- · Write and act out Scripture-based dramas or plays.
- · Establish family traditions that revolve around storytelling.

The only thing we can do wrong is not to try. Children aren't as much concerned about perfection as authenticity—by trying to connect, we're showing our love and being drawn into the Larger Story.

This, in the end, is what they'll remember, when all the dust has settled and all the books are closed.

Chapter 5

# Out-Romancing the Competition

*Kneeling by my children's bedside
In the light of the moon,
I know heaven is watchin'
And there's angels in this room.*

"ARROWS"

W hen I was an undergraduate studying geology, I saw a *National Geographic* cover showing a panoramic view of the North Cascade Mountains of Washington State. It dazzled me, haunting my imagination for months. The following summer I landed a job on the crest of the North Cascades—exactly where the photo had been taken. Our helicopter-supported camp was sixteen miles from the nearest road, with a spectacular view of the snowcapped volcanic mountain named Glacier Peak.

My assistant was an experienced technical rock climber and mountaineer. On our days off from climbing mountains for work we climbed mountains for fun—peaks with names like White Chuck, Bonanza, Ripsaw Ridge, Spiral Point, and Fourth of July.

I'll never forget the first technical climb we did up the

north face of Fortress Mountain. Days before the climb, we stared across the deep cirque just south of our camp, at the mountain's foreboding face, as we planned our route. During the climb I couldn't get over how cautious my assistant was. For the sake of safety, climbers sometimes connect themselves together with a rope. He wanted us to rope up almost all the time. It seemed like such a bother. The truth is that, in my ignorance and incompetence, I was a blind fool.

I soon learned that the most competent rock climbers are also the most cautious. They survive the dangers and make it to the top because they're prepared. They're conditioned and strong. They wear special boots and a helmet. They carry heavy packs loaded with survival gear, food, first-aid kits, sleeping bags, bivouac tents, ropes, carabiners, ice axes— everything they might possibly need. They predict the weather. They read the ice and the rock. They map out their route, concentrate, and get bruised and hungry, but they reach the summit. They're not only competent, they're alert and careful, because mountains can be deadly.

> We aren't the only ones who want to win our children's hearts; we have a rival with sinister designs.

In much the same way as I failed to take "roping up" seriously, we as parents can adopt too casual an attitude while raising our children. We fall into a foolish pattern of thinking: Everything will turn out fine. I see no "famine, war, or pestilence" on the horizon. Our children attend a "safe" school, our neighborhood is secure, our friends are Christians—all is well. There's nothing to worry about.

Arnie Burron says Ephesians 6:12 "ought to make us as

alert as we would be if we heard a news report that a psychotic child killer were stalking our neighborhood, looking for his next victim!"[20] Here's what that verse says: "For we do not wrestle against flesh and blood, but against principalities, against powers, against the rulers of the darkness of this age, against spiritual hosts of wickedness in the heavenly places."

We aren't the only ones who want to win our children's hearts. We have a rival, a suitor with sinister designs—the villain of our fairy tale. His name is Satan. Normally, we don't think of Satan as a "suitor." He's the enemy, described as a "roaring lion, seeking whom he may devour" (1 Peter 5:8). That makes us think of his frontal attacks—open spiritual warfare in which we must fight the devil for all we're worth. And these battles often do have a very real physical dimension, as our nation experienced on September 11, 2001.

But while we focus on the obvious battles, Satan lurks in the shadows, waiting for just the right moment to draw away our children's hearts, if he can. The apostle Paul exhorts Christians to "put on the whole armor of God, that you may be able to stand against the wiles of the devil" (Ephesians 6:11). Satan's "wiles" are tricks or stratagems intended to ensnare or deceive. The word implies skill in outwitting through trickery or guile, and it perfectly describes Satan's methods of trying to win our children. His objective is to deceive, entrap, and enslave the human heart—and the younger the better.

Many of us even see Satan as a caricature of cloven hoofs, horns, and a tail, wearing a red suit and carrying a pitchfork. The very persistence of this false image is strong evidence of his ability to deceive. He wants everyone to think he isn't real, or at least relatively harmless—the butt of costume-party humor. But the biblical view of Satan is far removed from all this. Satan was once a high angelic being, cast from heaven for rebelling against the Most High God. He can manifest himself as an angel of light. He can speak with eloquence and seem stunning in appearance. He's brilliant and knowledgeable, and he has a firm hold on our culture.

This complicates our efforts to romance our children's hearts to God. Yes, we can and should fight evil on all its fronts, as do many Christian parents and the organizations they support. For some people, their involvement in the fray seems like a modern holy crusade—with meetings, strategies, and other actions aimed at stemming the tide of evil and/or advancing the cause of truth, justice, and the Christian way. However, these well-meaning parents may never have considered that when they expend all their emotional, spiritual, and financial resources in righteous causes, they are, in effect, playing into Satan's hands. He knows that as long as he can keep them focused on barricading the front door, he can always slip in the back.

> *The devil's snares are a counterfeit of something God has already created.*

Our wily adversary doesn't war by the rules. Instead he conducts covert guerrilla warfare to pick off his victims one by one, by stealth, deception, trickery, and seduction.

## SNARES AND COUNTERFEITS

At some point, each of our children is going to be tempted by or subjected to ungodly influences, some of which we overlook, take for granted, perhaps even feel safe about—as I foolishly felt safe while climbing the face of that mountain. And when we feel most secure, our children may be most at risk.

The devil lures our children away through unsupervised television and videos, mindless computer games, unsupervised access to the Internet, some rock music and music videos, and questionable books and magazines. When our children spend time with friends, neighbors, and relatives we haven't checked out, Satan is there, lurking in the shadows. During those many hours when they participate in extracurricular activities after school, he waits. Sometimes even church youth group activities and Sunday school classes aren't exempt. Wherever our children may hear, "Your parents are just trying to keep you from having fun. Here, try this"— that's where the devil has the advantage.

When this happens, each child will face a choice: the way of wisdom or the way of folly. No set of rules, habits, or orthodox beliefs, not even the fear of eternal punishment, will compel a child to choose wisely. These factors operate from the outside in, usually originating in adults who tell children what they should believe and how they should act. If our children's faith is only outside-in, they'll almost surely fall into the snare of the devil.

In almost every case, the devil's snare is a counterfeit of something God has already created. God created man and woman to be one flesh in the beauty of passionate marital union. The devil perverts this into lust and promiscuity. God provides for our physical needs, giving us all things "richly to enjoy." Satan perverts this into gluttony and materialism. God instilled in us His creative image to bring us happiness and joy as we create. Satan monopolizes art and music in the name of fame and fortune.

The path of life is paved with counterfeits of all kinds. They beckon from the shadows, like the temptress in Proverbs, to come here or there and find what we've been missing. We cannot completely protect our children from this seduction. But we can out-romance the competition so our children will make the response that will keep their hearts in the day of testing. They'll be able to say, "I haven't been missing anything. I have all I need and more."

If we've won their hearts, their moral choices will come from the inside out, and making the right choice will be as natural as taking the next step on a path that leads toward God, not away from Him.

## OVERCOMING UNGODLY INFLUENCES

My parents' strategy regarding the ungodly influences we faced as kids was to do a kind of end run around them.

In my early teens, my artistic side was expressed in a passion for clothes. I loved to dress in a unique—some might even have said outrageous—way, including stunningly colorful Hawaiian shirts. Instead of fighting me tooth and nail about every item of clothing—which most of my friends' mothers were doing—Mom fought for my heart and won hands down. She took me to stores in downtown Milwaukee, far from where we lived, where I could find my "cool threads."

Despite being a fashion-setter of sorts, I struggled desperately with the subculture in junior high and high school. I didn't know how to be accepted and at the same time avoid the constant temptations and negative influences—dirty jokes on the school bus, miniskirts everywhere I turned, the petty politics of fitting into the in-crowd, and physical threats by young hoods.

> *Mom fought for my heart and won hands down.*

My father knew that idle time could be dangerous, so when I was fifteen he arranged for me to work with his crew as a carpenter's helper. While all my friends did odd jobs (or none at all), I was working with men, learning lifelong skills and developing a work ethic. I listened with them to their adult music—polkas, classical, big band—and learned much about respecting authority. One day the crew stapled me to the oak layout table—clothes, shoes, and all. My dad watched but didn't intervene, letting them tutor me in the sociology of his workplace.

My dad beat out the competition for my affection by setting before me a man-size challenge, believing I could do it, and mentoring me in the craft he knew best. He couldn't have given me a better gift.

They supported me as well in my high school commitment to basketball, which became more than a game to me; it was my primary arena of creative expression. When I wasn't playing basketball I was thinking about it. I trained with weights on my ankles and slept with a basketball. I made it my goal to earn a basketball scholarship for college, to save my parents' money as a way of saying thank you for all they'd invested in me. By the time I finished high school I held most of the school records, and I'd qualified for a college scholarship.

The most dramatic test of my parents' heart-winning

influence came when I was elected king of the senior prom. The prom would take me into Milwaukee's beer-drinking, Saturday-night-dancing culture—standards that didn't mesh with my family's fundamentalist values. I was torn between wanting to be accepted by my peers and wanting to please my parents, who made it clear I would have to make up my own mind.

In the end I turned down the honor because I didn't feel comfortable dancing anymore. That decision might have been different in another time and another culture, but it was right for me then. I knew by intuition and experience that the way of my parents—which had become my own way, even when it was difficult—was superior to anything or anyone else that might whisper my name. Interestingly, I found I had more friends after I made my decision known.

Although my parents had clear boundaries for us, they had few rules. Their boundaries were walls that didn't move, but we had freedom within them. I had no curfew, and I was given the responsibility to make my own moral choices. I was also burdened with the consequences; I knew they wouldn't rescue me from the results of my wrong choices, though they loved me no less for them.

## THE BEAUTY CONTEST

Out-romancing the competition to win our child's heart is more like a beauty contest than open warfare. In choices of the heart, a child will naturally be drawn to the most beautiful option. It's how we're created. "No man can live without delight," Thomas Aquinas said. Frederick Buechner said beauty is as essential to the spirit as food is to the body. We're empty without it. We're created in the image of the Creator, and we find happiness by bringing order out of chaos and making things of beauty—from poetry to pot holders.

Some Christians have a difficult time fitting beauty into their theology, because the culture we live in worships it. This is where Satan blindsides us, taking advantage of our negligence.

Edith Schaeffer relates a conversation with two African students at European universities who had earlier attended mission schools in Africa.

> They each made a similar comment which impressed me deeply. Each of them said that the thing which had turned them away from Christianity was the lack of beauty in the missionaries' homes—and they were speaking of physical beauty. The God of the universe they saw created a beautiful world, but they did not see this beauty radiating from these Christians' homes.[21]

You can imagine how these Africans, who lived close to God's creation, had been confused by an evangelistic message that wasn't more strongly connected to the beauty of that creation.

Beauty is profoundly part of God. In Scripture, God's beauty and glory can be described only indirectly, because it's so great. His divine presence is overwhelming—for God dwells "in unapproachable light" (1 Timothy 6:16).

My mother is an artist. The beauty she brought to my life drew me to God. She decorated our home with several original paintings because she wanted us to learn to appreciate the nuances of texture and color that couldn't be detected in reproductions. More, she believes we can understand the soul of the artist only through an original.

Two of these paintings now hang in my home. One was painted for my grandmother by a lumberjack. It's an oil rendition of a bull elk standing in a lake at the foot of a mountain, with tall spruce, willows, and granite rocks edging the water. Mom loved it because of her fascination with the Rocky Mountains—she named me "Monte" because it means "man from the mountains."

> *Many families find it hard to spend even a few minutes together each day—or week.*

Through the years I've lived this painted scenario many times as I pursued elk through the Rockies. I'm sure a painting encountered in youth can instill a vision in a child's heart that will last a lifetime.

My mother painted the other when she was in college. The simple pine frame, made by my grandfather, enhances the romantic image of two whitetail deer bounding down a snow-covered glacial hill. A lone white pine stands in memory of the great Wisconsin virgin forest, and several white birches stand in stark relief against the snow. The little boy who hugged the pine stump comes alive in me every time I look at that picture, for it connects me with my heritage—the brush strokes are my mother's, and the setting is God's creation.

The beauty my parents helped me see in creation gave me a sense of wonder that became the primary factor in my own passion for science.

## WINNING THE BUSYNESS BATTLE

Distraction is Satan's most common strategy, and the one he uses effectively. One of his favorite distraction strategies today is to fill our lives with so many good options and opportunities that many families find it hard to spend even a few minutes together each day—or week—because there's always somewhere else to go and something else to do. Our society's affluence has allowed these opportunities to grow exponentially.

When I went to high school in the late sixties, I had only one teenage friend who drove his own car to school. He had to park in the teachers' lot, because there wasn't another parking area. Today, one of our local high schools has three parking lots reserved just for students.

My younger son's shoes also demonstrate this point. Dawson has shoes for children's chorale, backpacking, running, mountain biking, church, ice skating, in-line skating, bowhunting, cross-country skiing, telemark skiing, canoeing, fishing, winter hiking, skin diving, fly-fishing, horseback riding, and more. The only reason he doesn't have a pair for tae kwon do—where he reached the black belt level at age twelve—is because he works out barefoot. These shoes, which overflow from his closet, reflect his life—filled to the brim with wonderful opportunities.

Myriad world-class recreational and other opportunities compete for our children's time, in the end threatening to possess them as basketball possessed me for seven years. Even with all the positive aspects of that involvement, I sometimes wonder what I missed by investing so much time, energy, and passion into playing with that round ball.

Besides the financial strain imposed by participation in competitive sports—including specialized equipment and training with experts—the other aspects require time. Usually mothers end up becoming nearly full-time chauffeurs.

Recently, Karey and I spoke at a conference and shared this challenge. Several days later a mother wrote and described a miracle that had taken place in her family. Her husband had returned home realizing he needed to turn off the TV and do productive things like Bible study with the kids. Even more miraculously, he decided their son would do only one sport next year. Her husband had a vision during the conference, involving being with his family so they could make maple syrup, plant gardens, and go fishing.

She said that although their son is highly athletic and loves sports, he responded to this change by saying, "Now we won't have to rush so much and we can just be at home and do stuff" —a comment that brought tears to his mother's eyes. In her letter she described watching her husband at home on a day off, tapping maple trees with the kids, pushing one of the girls on a swing, and building a fire outside.

The value judgments we're forced to make today are not easy. When we try to preserve our families, we see opportunities slipping away; when we seize the opportunities, we see our families slipping away. Satan finds enthusiastic support from our culture's childhood "experts" who contend that children need all these opportunities and that parents who withhold any of them are somehow negligent.

## WINNING THE INTELLECTUAL BATTLE

Another of Satan's strategies is to overwhelm our children's minds with secular ideas and deceptive logic, using the youth subculture to pressure them to become skeptics and cynical rationalists. He also applies pressure from the adult world by exposing them, as early as possible, to a variety of moral dilemmas beyond their capacity to understand.

There's much we can do to physically shield them from this exposure, but often their only protection is prayer. One day in late summer, our church decided to pray for and commission the college students of our congregation as they returned to their campuses. Words like "sending soldiers to war" and "they're warriors returning to a battle that's a life-and-death struggle" were said with sincere, heartfelt emotion.

These precious sons and daughters were in the process of flying the nest. The reality of moral dilemmas, temptation, and the clashing of worldviews flavored our supplications to God. As the prayers became more and more passionate, we adults examined our own hearts and our place in the spiritual battle. Empathizing with our young comrades, we felt a yearning to be with them on the front lines—standing alongside, shoulder to shoulder, dressing their wounds and guarding their flank. We feared for their minds, knowing that rationalistic professors would attempt to browbeat them for their faith. We covenanted together to uphold them in prayer throughout the school year.

As the prayer time was drawing to a close, someone spoke up: "What about our high school students? They're going into an intellectual and spiritual battle as well. Let's commission and pray for them, too." This was a little awkward—to think about sending high schoolers to war. But we prayed for them and it felt right.

Then someone said, "What about our junior high students?" The next logical thought was, "What about our grade school children...and we can't leave out our preschoolers."

At that moment everyone got the point—a lightning flash of truth straight from heaven striking our hearts. We were sending children to war! There was an awkward, guilty silence, and finally someone said "Amen" and, to everyone's relief, the normal part of the service began again. We wouldn't dream of sending children to war in the physical realm. But in the intellectual and spiritual realms, where so much more is at stake, such warfare is already a reality for them.

## RELATIONSHIP OVER MISSION

Even when we set aside time for protectively nurturing our relationship with our children, Satan can sneak in and distract us. He can contaminate the fellowship, sometimes by manipulating our agenda until it's at odds with our child's.

When Dawson was nine, I took him fishing along a beautiful little mountain stream near our home—a whole day fishing, just the two of us. For me, this stretch of stream held special memories. I'd taken Travis and Heather fishing there—in sunshine, in rain, through thick clouds of mosquitoes, sometimes carrying them on my back for miles. But we always caught fish and returned home with ravenous appetites and satisfied souls.

Dawson and I hiked about a mile and a half from the trailhead on the main trail, then hiked another half mile on a little-known path to a secret spot of mine. My goal was to fish our way up to a special pool my brother told me about, where he'd once lost a huge cutthroat trout. The pool lay at the base of a tumbling waterfall where a beaver had built a high dam. Because of its remoteness, it had grown larger in my imagination, almost to the point of enchantment.

Intent upon reaching it, I hurried Dawson along from one pool to the next as we moved upstream. When he managed to catch trout along the way, I hardly acknowledged them as he held them up for me to see. I even made

> *I destroyed the key to romancing his heart that day.*

him skip some pools. He was catching fish, but I didn't care. I was on a mission to reach my secret pool, where I wanted him to catch the biggest fish in the stream.

Instead of relating to Dawson—which was why I'd taken him fishing in the first place—I was having a relationship with a mission. And he felt it in his boyish heart. We should have been two kindred spirits out enjoying God's creation and each other's company. Instead, slowly but surely, I squandered the riches of my relationship with him and destroyed the key to romancing his heart that day.

It brings tears to my eyes now as I think about how I dragged him up that stream, sacrificing his sense of wonder on the altar of my mission.

Though Dawson's wonderful whimsical spirit resisted my prodding at first, he soon gave in. He tried his best to act excited when we reached my goal. But waters from the spring runoff had washed away the beaver dam, and the pool was gone—poetic justice for a father who had lost track of why he and his son were together in the first place.

Dawson seemed quieter than normal just before we headed back. It was late, so I decided to bushwhack it to the main trail to save some time. But that almost turned into a disaster as we ran into an old forest fire burn where young aspens had grown up so thick I could hardly squeeze through. Threading our fishing rods between them was a tedious challenge. And there were huge spruce logs to maneuver over, under, and around, and boulders everywhere. It was tough going, almost overwhelming for about a half mile.

Dawson kept falling behind. I was afraid we might get separated, so I had to stop often to wait for him. This wasn't normal—he's usually in the lead. Even when we broke out of the trees and began hiking down the main trail, he quietly shuffled along behind me while I carried his pack and fishing pole. I felt impatient and irritated.

That night at home we discovered he'd come down with chicken pox. He'd been sick and feverish all day, but I'd been too preoccupied with my fishing contest to notice.

But all wasn't lost. The Larger Story of our relationship told Dawson that this was just a small detour in our journey together.

A few weeks later we went fishing again. This time I let my little "Tom Sawyer" set the agenda and lead the way. We lingered for a long time at some holes and managed a fine catch. At the end of the day we ate crispy, golden brown pan-fried cutthroat trout, cooked over an open fire in a lush meadow of lilac purple fireweed under a clear blue sky—a moment of pure romance this father and son will never forget.

Perhaps, when Dawson is wooed by the other suitor, he'll even think of this experience, and others like it we've shared. When Satan comes knocking he'll be able to say, "No, thank you. There's nothing you could offer me that I don't already have."

As parents, just showing up for the contest is half the battle, and it's never too early—or too late—to begin. Children are so understanding and forgiving and, like Dawson, reluctant to remember it very long when we make a mistake. They're quick to see the good in us and to embrace it. (How sweet life would be if this were as true of adults!)

# Chapter 6

# The Watershed

*There's a way of wisdom*
*And a way of fools;*
*And the way of wisdom*
*Is straight and true.*

"STRAIGHT AND TRUE"

We live near the Continental Divide—the Rocky Mountain backbone of North America. When you stand on the Divide above the timberline at Loveland Pass (11,992 feet above sea level) and look east or west, peak after peak stretches out before you in a complex pattern of deeply carved glacial canyons.

In the late spring I've stood on a snowfield at the Divide, watching one rivulet of water flow east and another from the same snowfield flow west. The eastern rivulet will be captured by Clear Creek, which rushes straight down the Front Range, picking up and dropping gold along the way, until it joins the Platte River and from there flows into the Missouri and Mississippi Rivers. Finally, it reaches the Gulf of Mexico, from which it will be carried north by the Gulf Stream as a river of fresh water in the salty Atlantic Ocean, until it finally mixes into the North Atlantic somewhere west of Scandinavia.

The rivulet flowing westward will tumble down the North

Fork of the Snake River into Dillon Reservoir, where it will become part of the beautiful Blue River. Then it will join the Colorado River, which winds its way through Lake Powell, Lake Mead, and the Grand Canyon, until it's diverted into Central Arizona Project's aqueduct to serve the land and people needs of the water-starved desert of Arizona— never reaching the Gulf of California and the Pacific Ocean.

> Our "heartset" determines how we'll respond to the testings and temptations of life.

This is how two droplets of water, once part of the same snowpack, can end up thousands of miles apart in different worlds. The dividing line, in this case the Continental Divide, is called a watershed.

A crucial dividing line or turning point in a person's life is also called a watershed. God's rain falls on both the just and the unjust, as Jesus said, and that's true also for the "rain" of life— including adversity and temptations. Sometimes this rain has destructive results. Sometimes it simply waters the ground. But regardless of whether the "rain" is gentle or harsh, the direction the water follows after it hits is determined by a person's "watershed"—the "set" or established attitude of their heart.

The word set occurs in the Bible hundreds of times, often in relation to choices faced: the set of the mind, of the will, of the body, and of the heart. I'd like to make up a new word: heartset. The set of the heart in every child and adult determines how they'll respond to the testings and temptations of life.

One of my favorite Scriptures describes how Jesus "steadfastly set His face to go to Jerusalem" (Luke 9:51). Why? To endure the cross for the joy set before Him, which was the redemption of all who would trust in Him for their salvation. Jesus' face was set to take His body to Jerusalem, because His will was set, because His heart was set. Jesus' purpose in life was to be lifted up on the cross to draw all men to Himself, and His mind could not be changed, even when people like Peter tried to change it.

Until a certain point in life, a child's thoughts and actions more or less depend on parental values and control. Parents stand like buffers, protecting their children from life-impacting choices, offering guidance and correction when necessary.

As children near adulthood, they begin to think more independently, choosing the way of wisdom or the way of folly. These watershed choices will have dramatic consequences that are worlds apart.

Even a child of godly parents may go through periods of rebellion that leave the parents few options but to live by hope and faith, all the time praying for God's grace and wisdom. One of my minister friends recalls how, once he got away from home and into a Christian college, he wrote his parents (his father was also a minister) to say he no longer wanted to have anything to do with their God. Their response—beyond expressing their shock, concern, and dismay—was to let their son know they loved him and to acknowledge that this, indeed, was his choice alone and they would not interfere. They showed respect for him instead of trying to manipulate him toward the choice they desired for him.

Allowing this much freedom is difficult, especially for parents who have maintained close control for most of their child's life. Usually, the greater the pressure put on a child to decide, the greater the chance that the choice will not be for

God. But when God and His way of wisdom is an uncoerced choice, it will stand up to the tests of life.

## UNDERSTANDING A KEY PASSAGE

Proverbs 22:6 tells us: "Train up a child in the way he should go, and when he is old he will not depart from it." This verse is central to understanding the idea of Romance. Many Bible teachers interpret this passage to mean that the challenge to parents is to know their child well in order to train them according to their own "bents"—talents, abilities, spiritual gifts, and other unique God-given capabilities. I remember vividly how my parents applied this principle as they raised my brothers and me. They never hesitated to go out of their way in finding each of their son's individual bents, and in praising us equally in our different accomplishments.

However, it's the parents' responsibility to deal with the negative bents as well. Every archer knows that straightening a bent aluminum arrow takes time and patience. If you press too hard and too quickly on the bend, you'll break the arrow. If you don't press hard enough, you won't straighten the bend. To be successful you must give the straightening process your undivided attention, with just the right amount of pressure for as long as it takes.

Looking at this verse from a larger biblical perspective, we see that training a child includes the idea of starting a child along a particular way.[22] The word way is the walk of faith. In fact, the "Way" was the first name applied to the new movement that eventually was called "Christianity" (Acts 9:2). Even nonbelievers recognized that embracing Christ meant to adopt a new way of living.

In *You and Your Child,* Charles Swindoll explains that the original root of "train up" is the term for "the palate, the roof of the mouth, the gums." In the days of Solomon, this term described the action of the midwife. After a child was delivered, the midwife would dip her finger into chewed or crushed dates, then touch and massage the gums and palate of the infant to stimulate the sense of taste and the sensation of sucking. The baby would then be placed in the mother's arms to begin breast-feeding. So the expression "train up" also means to "develop or create a thirst."[23] Thus, "Train up a child in the way he should go" literally means to develop or create a thirst in the child so the child will start walking in the way he should go—in the way of wisdom.

There are two ways to create a thirst. The most common approach is behaviorist training, which causes someone to acquire a thirst for something he doesn't naturally desire. The goal of romance, by contrast, is that the child will develop a thirst based on desire. A balanced combination of these two approaches is the proper biblical approach.

> *The crucial issue for parents is whether we're walking in the way of wisdom ourselves.*

Starting a child along the way is theologically pivotal to romancing his heart, which comes after the thirst is created. We cannot simply place a child along the way as we would place him on a path to start walking. To be "along the way" means we're moving—it's a process, and process involves choosing which way to go.

As a child breast-feeds, bonding occurs, and eventually

mother and child know each other through this intimate experience. Security and serenity are reflected in the child's eyes as he gazes on his mother's face. Trust is established between parent and child.

Once trust is gained, a child allows himself to be carried along the way on the shoulders of his parent's faith—a simple but important early training in choosing well. Their journey together introduces the Larger Story, which is filled with delight, challenge, mystery, and beauty, revealing the character of Christ in the parents' hearts through both good and difficult times. Ultimately this leads to a personal encounter with the Story's almighty Author—God Himself.

Until I was seven, I thought my father was God. Once I discovered this wasn't true, I began to look for the real God—my father had projected the image of God so accurately, genuinely, and positively that I wanted to know Him personally. At age eight, I asked the Lord into my life during an Awana meeting.

Our first desire as parents is that our children will receive Jesus Christ as their personal Savior. To me, the phrase "when he is old he will not depart from it" implies that a child who has started along the way of wisdom will one day climb down from their parents' shoulders of faith and continue by their own faith to walk along that path.

As this watershed event approaches, the crucial issue for parents isn't what we know (although this is important) or how skilled we are at walking (though this also is important), but whether we're actually walking in the way of wisdom ourselves. Only then can we hope to start a child along this way. I'm not saying we must be perfect, for God's grace covers our humanness. The result is determined not by our performance but by our dependence on His Spirit to work through us and in our child.

Parents may try, sometimes desperately, to make their children conform to the way of wisdom. But while a child may be forced to comply, no one can be forced to love. As George Strait sings,

> *You can't make a heart love somebody;*
> *You can tell it what to do,*
> *But it won't listen at all.*
> *You can't make a heart love somebody;*
> *You can lead it to love,*
> *But you can't make it fall.*[24]

We find our temporal and eternal identity, purpose, and fulfillment in relationship, with God and with others. Relationship is the web of meaning that connects all the components of our lives, enabling us to be whole physically and spiritually. It isn't necessarily related to the amount of biblical doctrine crammed into our heads, or to how well our behavior has been controlled by our parents. These efforts will be of little value without the child's willing heart. Navigators founder Dawson Trotman said, "Discipline imposed from the outside eventually defeats when it is not matched by desire from within."[25]

This inward desire, capable of producing personal discipline from the inside out, can come only from love. We were made by Love and for love. We don't love God because we must, but because "He first loved us" (1 John 4:19).

We love God because He has romanced our hearts to

Himself—through others, through creation, and through the cross.

## THE ORIGINS OF ROMANCE

The word romance first appeared in southern France in the twelfth century as the vernacular Latin word romaz. Later, usage spread to Italy and Spain. The verb to romance described the process of wooing, drawing, or attracting for the purpose of winning the heart.

> *In our culture's eyes, the biblical romance is a simpleminded fairy tale, and its Hero just a fool on the hill.*

As a noun, romance described an extravagant story about the winning of a heart, usually characterized by extraordinary adventure, chivalry, beauty, sacrifice, unconditional love, and the passions of wonder and curiosity. This type of story vaulted beyond the natural to the supernatural, soaring above the limits of empirical facts to ultimate truth as it dealt with the deepest matters of the heart. Romances were often sophisticated and psychologically insightful, and had happy endings—the romanced heart was won. Descriptive details were lavish in presenting exotic, remote, and miraculous adventure. Often a romance emphasized drama and human character, and the long-suffering of the romancer. Medieval authors (A.D. 1100–1400) wrote some of the greatest romances—such classics as the original tales of King Arthur and the knights of the Round Table.

The Romantic Movement developed in the 1700s and

early 1800s. Romanticism emphasized passion rather than reason, and imagination and emotion rather than logic. It developed as a revolt against restrictive social and artistic conventions and against unjust political rule. The gothic romances were written from this perspective. Romances by Sir Walter Scott and James Fenimore Cooper are famous examples. Although this type of romance literature wasn't usually about the winning of a heart, some works preserved this feature—for example, the powerful Les Misérables by Victor Hugo, a great story about grace versus justice.

Our current culture's concept of romance has grown largely out of a naturalistic worldview in which there is no Creator—therefore no Author, no Hero, and no Larger Story. We're only a product of time, chance, and matter—biochemical entities alone in a universe ruled by chaos. Romance in the spiritual sense, therefore, cannot exist. Consequently, in our culture's eyes, the biblical romance is a simpleminded, naive fairy tale, and its Hero just a fool on the hill.

Another important factor in our culture is relativism: No truth is absolute, and reality is what we wish it to be. We all have the right to make up our own truth or create our own reality, as long as we don't force anyone else to accept it. This philosophical anarchy leads adherents directly into the lair of the great liar, Satan.

Toleration is the law where relativism reigns, except that the following claims are not tolerated: Truth really does exist; some things are really real; some things are truly good (therefore, some are evil); God really does exist; and it's good to teach these things to our children. In our culture's eyes, we who long to romance our children to God and His way of wisdom are guilty of brainwashing our own children—tantamount to child abuse. We're arrogant "cultists" whose families are at risk to a degree that warrants government intervention.

Relativism is the antithesis and enemy of romance. Our culture stereotypes romance negatively, writing off any movie as "just a chick flick" if the main theme is human romance or relationship.

> *Romance concerns relational truth more than propositional truth.*

Although romance may appear to be an elastic word with many historical nuances, the genuine article is easy to recognize. Romance emanates from personality; it's not passive but flows out of a person in such qualities as beauty, order, humor, peace, unconditional love, compassion, hope, enthusiasm, happiness, enchantment, and respect. "Big Story" romantics know their destination is heaven; they can't help but be full of smiles and joy.

By contrast, unromantic people are characterized by confusion, despair, dullness, fear, tension, boredom, skepticism, and cynicism—an inner deadness that sucks the life out of people around them. If there's a story in their lives, it's a tragedy from start to finish. Their hearts are hidden, held close and protected from the risks of relationship. They're strangers even to themselves. Most of their knowledge is theoretical and secondhand. They live from day to day without hope, and they seldom smile.

Most of us live somewhere between these extremes, swinging toward one or the other. For our children's sake we need to spend as much time as we can at the romantic end. But we cannot put on romantic characteristics like garments—

they must come from the inside. If we want to romance our children's hearts, the truly pivotal watershed decision is our own. Do we yearn for a relationship with God characterized by firsthand knowledge and passionate love? Or are we content to know God in a theoretical, secondhand way?

A friend once asked me why romancing a child's heart is such a remote concept. I pondered this for months until I realized "romance" is not a concrete term. It concerns relational truth more than propositional truth. We look for a formula, but romance is an abstract concept—the "smile of the heart."

Even as adults, we can be romanced to God. We can allow His love to penetrate our hearts like an arrow—not from the bow of Cupid, but from Christ.

## THE ORIGINAL ROMANCER

In *The Sacred Romance,* Brent Curtis and John Eldredge propose that our relationship with God is actually a love affair—a grand eternal Story or Romance.

It's not an intellectual relationship that centers on ideas, doctrines, theology, dogma, and "righteous" fulfillment of all the rules. The relationship God desires with you and me is an affair of the heart—an eternally passionate Romance written before time began.

Our Creator's passion and longings for us resound from Genesis to Revelation, depicted in the image of a bridegroom rejoicing over his bride. Because God is resolved to guard this "marriage" against attack, His jealousy is a positive virtue; He's grievously offended if His lover is inclined toward a rival, and burns with hottest fire: "For the LORD, whose name is Jealous, is a jealous God" (Exodus 34:14).

His intensely emotional love for us pulsates throughout the prophets: "For your Maker is your husband.... Though the mountains be shaken and the hills be removed, yet my unfailing love for you will not be shaken" (Isaiah 54:5, 10, NIV). He tells us, "I have loved you with an everlasting love" (Jeremiah 31:3).

When His bride runs away from Him, He pursues us and agonizes over her rejection, and affirms, "Therefore I am now going to allure her; I will lead her into the desert and speak tenderly to her" (Hosea 2:14, NIV).

This passionate relationship between God and His people is illumined in a striking way in the Song of Songs, which portrays romantic human love with all its longing, sadness, beauty, and joy. It also gives a high view of human sexual love and companionship, describing it in terms of sensual beauty and wonder—even using the language of romantic fantasy. The imagery the author uses may seem almost embarrassingly intimate to the practical, rational Christian.

> Grace is
> at the center of
> the Sacred
> Romance.

But the primary value I see in Song of Songs is that it elegantly legitimizes romance, placing this wonderful and dangerous realm into the spiritual context of the other dimensions of God's love that the Bible as a whole reveals. Song of Songs suggests that human love provides a way of understanding God's love: God delights in us, gives Himself to us, desires us wholly for Himself, and feels deeply both the pain and pleasure of relationship with us.

God desires lovers, not guilt-driven moralists or Pharisees.

He has gone to extravagant lengths to win our hearts. This is clearly seen not only in the Scripture but also in creation, a gift God made to dazzle us. As we smell a wildflower in the springtime, watch a blazing sunset over the desert, or witness a thunderstorm on a sultry summer afternoon, beauty and drama capture our hearts. Is the wonder we feel the response He hoped for as He created these things?

I'm confident that creation reveals another aspect of romance in God's heart. He's the first Quilter of prairies, the prime Painter of autumn colors, the archetypical Sculptor of mountains, the master Composer of the whippoorwill's song, and the original Poet of grace and truth. And He has imprinted His creative image in human hearts. Burning curiosity, wonder at mystery, and delight at finding a solution that makes order visible—all these accompany creativity, giving us our fullest happiness and deepest satisfaction on earth.

Are the five senses He created in us specially intended for experiencing His creation—an extravagant gift of the Lover to His beloved? Could even time have been created to show us the heart of a long-suffering, patient Lover—who gives us chance after chance as He longs for us to come home?

One additional word, which Philip Yancey has described as "the last best word," incarnates romance. Nothing captures the essence of God's romance with us better than the word grace.

Grace is nearly synonymous with romance. It's at the center of the Sacred Romance. It demands nothing from us but that we shall await it. Grace always comes "free of charge," Yancey says, "no strings attached, on the house"; grace is "a gift that cost everything for the Giver and nothing for the recipient."[26]

## NOT JUST ANY RELATIONSHIP

If we joyfully embrace God and His gracious, romantic love, knowing this love cost Jesus everything and us nothing, we'll be drawn into a love deeper than any human ever imagined—the perfect love experienced within the Trinity. Jesus spoke of this love as it relates to us when He prayed "that they all may be one, as You, Father, are in Me, and I in You; that they also may be one in Us" (John 17:21).

There's something here so basic to reality, so much a part of us, we may tend to overlook it. God is interested in not just any relationship. He's interested in the kind of relationship found within the Trinity, and God apparently created marriage as a physical symbol of this spiritual reality that Paul refers to as "a great mystery" (Ephesians 5:32). Jesus prayed: "Holy Father, keep through Your name those whom You have given Me, that they may be one as We are" (John 17:11). We may not be able to fathom what "one as We are" really means, but it certainly implies the greatest intimacy in relationship, within the context of unconditional love. Through being loved by God, and loving Him, we discover answers to life's most perplexing questions: How did I come to exist? What is my purpose? And what's it all about, anyway?

It's all about love. God is love. And because this is His essential nature, He created humanity to share this with Him.

"And now abide faith, hope, love, these three," Paul tells us; "but the greatest of these is love" (1 Corinthians 13:13). Philosopher Peter Kreeft says that, besides being greatest in value, love is also the greatest in size—that love is the meaning of the whole. Love is greater because it contains all the rest.

Before the world existed, the Father, Son, and Holy Spirit enjoyed unbroken loving relationship. Jesus said, in His prayer to the Father, "You loved Me before the foundation of the world" (John 17:24). We get a small glimpse of this indescribable fellowship when we sit around a dinner table or a campfire with close Christian friends and family. As we experience this fellowship, time stands still and we're immersed in the present—which is the only way to touch eternity, since God exists in the eternal present as the great I Am. Such experiences are among the highest joys we can know on earth, as our souls mysteriously connect with each other and with God.

> Our personal relationship with God makes us legitimate and believable to our children.

According to atheism, there's only human monologue, because there is no God and we're alone. According to pantheism, there's only divine monologue, for all is God. Only with theism is there dialogue between God and us, and communion both horizontally and vertically. As Kreeft points out, it's no accident that poetry and love songs, the product of romance, are written mainly in theistic cultures.

All creation flows from the triune fellowship—all of life, all of history. We're created with the potential to share this perfect intimacy and relationship, and God has placed within each human heart a longing for it. St. Augustine described it as a God-shaped vacuum—an innate knowledge that we were made for something more. The central, underlying principle of the universe is not about survival, chaos, or chance, but about intimate relationship—with our Creator, who loves us more than words can say and has been wooing us to Himself since before the beginning of time.

When this divine Romance of our hearts becomes real for us, when its passion penetrates our minds to our souls and we allow it to move us emotionally, it will flow from our inner self like a stream of refreshing, life-changing water, to everyone with whom we have a relationship— including our children.

## HEART-TO-HEART REALITY

Many Christians have looked to a particular passage in Deuteronomy as a blueprint for parenting:

> And these words which I command you today shall be in your heart. You shall teach them diligently to your children, and shall talk of them when you sit in your house, when you walk by the way, when you lie down, and when you rise up. You shall bind them as a sign on your hand, and they shall be as frontlets between your eyes. You shall write them on the doorposts of your house and on your gates. (Deuteronomy 6:6–9)

We gravitate toward these things to "do" because they define a clear, straightforward list. In biblical times the Jews took this passage literally, and actually tied little boxes containing these verses on their arms and foreheads, and fastened them on their doorposts. This approach simplified their lives by compartmentalizing these truths.

Instructing our children in disciplines and imparting

knowledge to them throughout the day seems to be the most obvious way to apply these verses to parenting. But the key to successful teaching of God's truth is the state of our hearts, which must be so permeated with the truth that what we teach is an overflowing of our relationship with God—not merely a repetition of correct ideas. "These words shall be in your heart," this passage says. Effective parental doing flows from being.

As fallen men and women we're naturally drawn to legalism. Relationship with a living person is less comfortable than operating by a formula or a to-do list. Legalism makes primary matters secondary and secondary matters primary. The legalistic conscience is haunted by a vague uneasiness about ever being in a right relationship with God—which is why the Pharisees invented ever more convoluted ways in which to fulfill the law of God. Legalists want to feel safe with God, but the closer they approach Him the less safe He appears.

Only our personal relationship with God makes us legitimate and believable to our children. Without it, our overtures will not be on pitch and our words will sound hollow. We can romance a child without having a relationship with God, but in that case we'll be romancing him to such things as materialism, legalism, agnosticism—effectively conducting him into the grip of the other suitor, Satan.

Romancing our child's heart requires heart-to-heart contact, and both hearts must be open and receptive. What a child reads in his parent's heart is the key unlocking the door to either a heavenly romance or an earthly tragedy.

## LIVING IN THE PRESENT

The Hebrews in the wilderness collected their manna every day. They weren't allowed to store it up because God wanted them to depend on Him for their daily needs. He wanted them to live in the present. The proof of our genuine relationship with the living God is found in our daily gathering of His sweetness, His Story, and His beauty in a world that can be bitter, cold, and tragic. Like Israel in the wilderness, we must learn to live in the present—in moment-by-moment relationship with the One who lives in the eternal present.

In the present we touch eternity through our relationship with Christ. This is what enables us to give not only to our children, but also to anyone else He brings into our lives. And the giving doesn't diminish us, for the refreshment others receive is from the stream of His living water welling up from within our souls.

At any given moment, our children can sense whether we're having a firsthand relationship with God, because long before children can read words they can read hearts. And romance happens because it comes through us from the Spirit of God.

A mother once told me she'll never completely fill the "gaps" in her parenting. But she has realized they provide the opportunity for Christ to shine through so the child sees only Christ, not her failures. In truth, the "perfect" parent with no gaps is in a sense a Pharisee, not giving Christ an opportunity to shine.

The good news is that any parent who wants to can meet with God at any time. Jesus said, "Behold, I stand at the door and knock. If anyone hears My voice and opens the door, I will come in to him and dine with him, and he with Me" (Revelation 3:20). This isn't so much a passage about how to be saved as how to have true fellowship with Him. I love the context—sitting around a table sharing a meal and sharing life. I trust this is what we all want for ourselves and our children.

Will you open that door to Him?

*Lord, You know the heart of the parent reading these words.*
*We long to know You and Your love more personally and passionately,*
*a love that heals all wounds, forgives all failures, and lifts every burden,*
*filling each heart with joy and a peace that passes all understanding.*
*May this day-to-day experience of Your love become a continual well-*
*spring of love for others, especially the children You have placed within*
*our care. Draw them to Yourself, through us, and may we always*
*help and never hinder this result. Amen.*

## Part Two

# Romancing Your Child
# ~ The Strategy ~

*I long most of all to be like the story*
*of a man I read about,*
*who shunned ivory palaces*
*to cook a meal on the beach with his buddies.*
*I can see him more clearly than ever before*
*in my mind's eye:*
*my squatting, smiling, fish-frying friend*
*who serves up his food on paper plates,*
*like the kingly feast that it is.*
*Our supper is very plain, yes.*
*We eat the bread of wonder.*

FROM "Give Us This Day Our Wonder Bread"

BY Joy Sawyer

# Chapter 7

# Requirements for Romance

*'Cause children's hearts are tender,*
*That's just the way they're made,*
*They're sent to us from heaven,*
*They stay a few short days.*

"STRAIGHT AND TRUE"

Our daughter, Heather, was adventurous and outgoing as a little girl. She gave unsolicited advice to adults in the grocery store, captured the lead role in musical dramas, and dreamed of becoming a race car driver when she grew up. She was a fearless skier—she always stood up when she shushed down a hill, while Travis, who's now an expert downhill skier, always sat down.

As with most children, the line between fantasy and reality was blurred, and her unhindered creativity took her on many adventures. Several times she ventured out alone on wilderness treks and got lost. One I'll never forget occurred during a new moon on a warm summer's night in the mountains west of Tucson, Arizona. That night you couldn't see your hand in front of your face. We had some guests over for dinner, and while we were distracted, Heather disappeared into the night, wearing flip-flops and shorts.

The Sonoran Desert is alive on summer nights. Mountain lions, scorpions, rattlesnakes, javelinas, Gila monsters, and a host of other creatures are out looking for a meal. Even now I cringe when I think of Heather walking through that jungle of cactus and over the sharp volcanic rocks surrounding our house. It was hard enough to navigate there in daylight without being stuck, stabbed, poked, punctured, or pricked. I had no idea where she'd gone, and when we called her there was no answer. How I found her an hour later I don't really know, but without doubt our confident, determined little Heather had a very special—and very busy—guardian angel.

> A child's heart is like a garden.

So when Heather became shy and timid at about ten, and her physical growth seemed to be slowing down, we took her to a growth specialist. He did many tests and concluded nothing was wrong, except that Heather's developmental pattern didn't match the usual bell curve. Her development was normal for her, but she would be a late bloomer—about three years late, based on an X ray of Heather's hand—and we should expect her cognitive and emotional development to follow a similar course. The specialist added, "You should try to enjoy Heather's extralong childhood. Kids grow up too fast these days anyway. One day they're little, the next they're in college."

We also took Heather to an educational specialist, who shared with us a simple but powerful metaphor. She told us Heather was like a rosebud. If we pulled the petals apart before they were ready to open, we would bruise and damage the rose. But if we waited patiently, the flower would open according to its own timing and become the sweet and beautiful rose God had planned. We followed her advice and her prediction came true—Heather has blossomed into a special, sweet, beautiful adult.

I'll never forget the day Heather laid aside her dog-eared Berenstain Bears storybook to pick up a historical novel. Just as the doctor had predicted, she moved from one stage to the next almost overnight. Had we forced the issue earlier just because Heather was "too old" for her bear books, we would have frustrated her, quenching her spirit and wounding her heart—bruising and damaging the flower. Knowing her timetable enabled us to protect her heart, giving it time to develop and ultimately giving us access to it.

A child's heart isn't a container into which you pour romance at your convenience. A child's heart is more like a garden. The soil needs to be cultivated, and the timing must be right. Fertile soil takes time to develop—to be ready to receive seed. And then, as love takes root, it must be protected and nurtured.

Too often we rush in, caught up in the busyness and complexity of life, expecting our children to follow the timetable of our particular romance agenda. It's like planting seeds out of season in soil that's untilled and not fertile. Whether we like it or not, there's a window of opportunity for romance that's open for a specific time—and then it closes.

## KNOWING THE STAGES OF YOUR CHILD'S DEVELOPMENT

A refusal to over-accelerate our children's development is one of the requirements for romancing them. More than a decade ago, David Elkind wrote *The Hurried Child: Growing Up Too Fast Too Soon,* in which he criticized our culture's speeded-up approach to raising children. He warned about parenting trends that result in "fourth graders dieting to fit into designer jeans and children of divorce asked to be the confidants of their troubled parents."[27]

For many parents, their own overbusy lifestyle is behind their rush to get their children grown up. One or both parents work long hours, returning home exhausted and stressed over ever-mounting debt, while convincing themselves they're doing it so their children can have the latest gadgets, gizmos, games, and toys. The children are left to raise themselves. Or rather, to be raised by things—television, videotapes, video games, MTV, the Internet.

Elkind says that such an assault on children produces hurried and stressed children who "mimic adult sophistication while secretly yearning for innocence."

To avoid this tendency to steamroll our children's maturity, it helps to remember that every child's development can be roughly divided into three stages.

During the first stage, the child is primarily an emotional being. The senses, coordination, and cognitive ability are developing and coming together, but aren't in balance. The child isn't ready to assimilate a heavy diet of facts or to face serious moral dilemmas. Often, simple things such as low blood sugar just before a meal will profoundly affect their personality. Peer pressure and highly structured academics are likely to damage a child who hasn't progressed beyond this developmental stage.

If this first hurdle is ignored, a child's wonder, creativity, and curiosity can be starved, stifled, and possibly crushed before they reach third grade. The childlike nature may become adultish, defensive, and cynical.

Children who are rushed through this stage lose their fluidity of mind, and their spirits shrink, pull inside, and close. For example, children forced to read before they're developmentally ready commonly have lifelong reading problems.

The second stage (5–7 to 11–13) begins when the child's senses and coordination come together. Typically, this correlates with being ready to read, to handle some academic structure and limited peer pressure. The child continues to be an emotional creature and has a difficult time understanding such things as winning, losing, and goal setting.

> *Genuinely sensitive parents will naturally know their child—they will listen, watch, and touch.*

The line between fantasy and reality is often blurred, and the imagination soars high and free. Broad exposure to nature and life through actual physical experience and good books is strongly recommended. (This is the stage in which our daughter remained several years longer than her age-mates.)

In the third stage (11–13 to 24–30), the child makes the transition from an emotional to a cognitive being. It's marked by the body's ultimate balancing act—the balancing of the two lobes of the brain and the development of the corpus callosum, the nerve connection between the brain's two lobes. This usually occurs between ages eleven and thirteen and is often accompanied by what's referred to as an "adolescent crisis." New studies show that this maturation is occurring later—sometimes not until between the ages of nineteen and thirty. Stress is thought to cause this delay.

Until this process is complete, an intense focus on goals, competition, and moral dilemmas (some within families, though many come from movies and TV) is confusing and detrimental to the child's development. Ignoring the importance of this developmental transition can cripple a child's spirit and cause chronic low-grade stress that may become a lifelong pattern.

## TUNED-IN ATTENTIVENESS

Another requirement for romancing your child is the kind of attentiveness in which parents become the student of their child. They make it a daily priority to concentrate consciously on each child.

Genuinely sensitive parents will naturally know their child—they will listen, watch, and touch. They're capable of sensing minute changes because all their senses are tuned in to their child's physical, emotional, sociological, and spiritual status. They're aware of the child's needs and interests, joy or pain.

One developmental factor in my children that I became particularly sensitive to concerns vision. This is an especially critical factor because of how it connects and relates such other developmental factors as verbal development, auditory-verbal match, and sensory-motor skills.

When one of our sons began to endure many headaches, we took him to the local pediatrician, who said the cause was probably diet or eyestrain. We then took him to an optometrist, who had a special interest in childhood development. He discovered that our son's eyes converged objects closer than the actual distance of the objects he was focusing on, so he was tending to see double. This caused him to do more neurological work than normal, as his brain tried to bring the double image together. It tired him out and eventually caused headaches. He now has reading glasses with prism lenses allowing his eyes to relax as he reads. He says the page is clearer and he doesn't get sleepy anymore. He's also doing visual perception developmental exercises, which strengthen the eyes to solve the convergent problem so that he won't need glasses in the future.

Not discovering this one thing could have had profound implications for our son's education—and his life. Improper convergence causes a whole array of symptoms, such as day-dreaming, short attention span, and headaches, and it forces a child to waste energy by compensating with the other senses. Fortunately, because of my own experience as a child, I was able to recognize our son's problem before damage occurred.

Sometimes, however, even normally sensitive parents can act insensitively.

One summer we decided to take a two-week whirlwind tour of Wyoming, Montana, Utah, and Colorado. Our vision was to give our two oldest children in particular an overview of all the national parks and monuments of the region, so the trip involved many short stops with long periods of driving in between.

We set out confidently and everything seemed to be going well, although stopping at nearly every road cut to let our nine-year-old son, Dawson, collect rocks, wood, and bones was slowing us down and turning our vehicle into a traveling museum. Although this matched our strategy of using creation to romance his heart to God, we eventually decided to curtail his explorations to save time.

Soon after we made that decision, we noticed Dawson seemed to be struggling with something. I watched him in the rearview mirror as we drove—his face contorted and his body straining to get loose from the seat belt. We tried to reason with him, but it didn't help much. His brain didn't seem to be connected with his heart. It reminded me of the difficulty I'd experienced sitting at a desk in a grade school classroom, hour after hour, year after year. Dawson's struggle came and went in waves. Soon he lost his desire to look out the window and even refused to look at the sights. He began giving his older brother and sister trouble. Such behavior wasn't normal for him.

At the end of a very long drive, we stopped at the North Rim of the Grand Canyon. Dawson didn't even want to look over the edge, and we had a difficult time keeping him on the trail. At Lake Powell, after another long drive, he disobeyed us as we let him out for a couple of minutes to look over the rim of the canyon at the water a thousand feet below. He took off running and wouldn't stop when we called. This was blatant defiance and I knew it was time to discipline him. But I felt terrible because I suspected we were causing the problem.

Ironically, we had stopped during this trip to speak at a conference in Utah, where we presented our ideas about romancing your child's heart. We urged the parents there to be sensitive to their children. We described teaching from the inside out instead of from the outside in. We had even used Dawson as an example of a hands-on learner who loves to explore and experience nature.

With his kinesthetic learning style and adventuresome spirit, Dawson longed to touch, taste, smell, and hear what the rest of us were content to see mostly through the car window as we whirled on by. Dawson needed to experience God's creation as much as he needed to eat. He was hungry for it, and frustrated because our trip thus far had been like taking a tour of a cafeteria, pausing only from time to time for a few tiny bites of the tantalizing food.

Soon after I realized more clearly the dynamics of all this, I spied a mountainside of layered sedimentary rocks. Dawson and I took on that mountain with rock hammers in hand and empty packs on our backs, while the rest of the family sat in the vehicle reading and watching the naturalists explore. The naturalists, meanwhile, were discovering that each layer was filled with fossils and rocks with fascinating color and texture.

> *To achieve heart-to-heart intimacy with a child, we must be there with our whole being.*

Dawson was transformed in those few minutes into a serious young scientist—a mature adult in miniature. I was in awe of my little boy. His enthusiasm was contagious and made the experience wonderful. Coming down with his pack, pockets, and arms full of rocks, Dawson began hypothesizing and sharing the geologic history of the mountain with us all. His older brother and sister just smiled; the real Dawson had returned. He was satisfied for a long time after that. And whenever we sensed he was "hungry" again, we stopped and let him "feast" on creation.

## TIME FACTORS

Another requirement that goes along with focused attentiveness in romancing your child is simply that of time—both
quality and quantity time.

Sometimes a child may need an entire day with us before
they'll share what's really on their heart. If your experience is
like mine, this tends to happen during the last few minutes of
the drive home together. Why do they wait so long? This is the
rhythm of relationship. If our timing is off and we ignore the
rhythm, we miss the music, repudiate the relationship, and
pass right by their heart.

Is a whole day with them too high a price to pay for a few
minutes of heart-to-heart conversation? Not on your life.
Sensitivity requires patience, patience requires time, and time
together is the stuff relationships are made of.

To achieve heart-to-heart intimacy with a child we must
be there with our whole being, not just physically while our
minds are distracted. The greatest challenge for some parents
in the romance of their child's heart is simply to show up.
Fathers in particular have this problem, because they tend to
have narrow focus. They're wired this way and for good reason—their traditional roles include protector and provider for
the family. But when they're overly focused and miss important moments and opportunities to be with their child, this
strength becomes a weakness. Just try to have a conversation
with a man who's watching television. Chances are he won't
even notice you're there.

Despite working long hours, my dad put relationship first
and spent time with his sons. He attended every basketball

game we played (nearly five hundred in all). He took us on trips from coast to coast so we could experience America first-hand. He made us a baseball diamond with a huge backstop fashioned from telephone poles he split by hand. To hold the things we were always collecting, he built shelves and drawers in our bedrooms. As we grew older he allowed us to help him with certain projects, sometimes stepping back to let us work things out ourselves.

For Karey and me, one of our best provisions for family togetherness grew out of a comment made by a close friend and mentor of mine, Gene Swanson. "All our major family decisions were made around a campfire," he told me. Gene had a well-used fire pit encircled with stones near his home. It was also rigged with traditional cast-iron utensils that had been used to cook many wonderful meals.

We caught this vision from Gene and have built our own fire pit, cradled in a natural amphitheater just below our house. I staked logs into the concave hillside for seating. Two aspen trees serve as sentinels, and the evening thermals always flow downhill, carrying the wood smoke away from where we sit.

> *Children are sensitive and emotional beings— not cognitive adults.*

A campfire demands narration and response from those sitting around it. Everyone has a story as the circle of light and warmth draws us in out of the darkness. We feel far from the distractions of our urgent world. We aren't on a stage— expected to perform; we're just here, now, together. Campfires magically create a sense of camaraderie and community in the people encircling the fire, from children to adults, providing a setting where the deepest communication can occur, not merely through words but intuitively, through feelings—the connector of human hearts.

## FILLING THEIR EMOTIONAL TANKS

Children are sensitive and emotional beings—not cognitive adults. Their fund of knowledge is small and they communicate primarily through their feelings. The eyes of the heart determine how they perceive family members, their home, their friends, and the world. They need to feel they're loved unconditionally, not just know it. They need to touch our love, hold it in their hands, and sense how much it's theirs. This gives them emotional wholeness.

Children use behavior to communicate their feelings, and they recognize our feelings by our behavior. They're more skillful at this than adults because they're less distracted. We think our words have power in themselves to communicate our feelings to our children, because we underestimate our children's ability to "listen" to the way we behave. They read between the lines and they're watching us all the time.

Children are naturally generous. They give freely when their emo-

> *Punishing a child for anything apart from purposeful disobedience is risky.*

tional tanks are full; only then can they be expected to be moved by our romance. There's rarely an exception to this, for children are by nature responsive even to the feeblest adult attention. But if we don't fill their tanks, they'll eventually get them filled somewhere else, and possibly respond to another—a false—romance.

Gary Chapman in his book on the love languages shares five ways parents can fill their children's emotional tanks: words of affirmation, quality time, giving gifts, acts of service, and physical touch.[28] In order to keep our children's emotional tanks fillable, we must avoid poking holes in them by overreacting to childish behavior that may on the surface appear to be defiance. As long ago as 1978, Dr. James Dobson wrote, "Our objective [as parents] is not only to shape the will of the child...but to do so without breaking his spirit."[29] Nothing breaks the spirit of a child faster than punishing him for acting like a child.

When Dawson was four years old, he built a fort out of pillows in our parlor. At the end of the day Karey went to help him put the pillows back in their proper places. She reached down to pick up the first pillow and it wouldn't move. She tried another, then another. They were all nailed through the carpet into the subfloor! She just stood there in amazement—then laughed and even praised Dawson for his creativity, after helping him understand this wasn't good for the pillows or the carpet. He has never done it again. She often shudders as she imagines how she would have reacted had this happened when our older children were young, when she was less experienced and knowledgeable about a child's creativity, spirit, and will.

Our older children probably never would have thought of doing anything like that. They're simply wired differently from Dawson. I suspect that, had they done the same thing, it would have been an act of defiance. There are some difficult judgments a parent must make, but I would rather err on the side of grace by interpreting such actions as childishness. I would rather overprotect than underprotect their spirits.

Punishing a child for anything apart from purposeful disobedience is risky. In fact, how we respond to offensive behavior or misbehavior in our children reflects on us and judges us. Are we responding to their behavior or to their hearts?

As a boy, I always knew there were certain "lines in the sand" my parents drew that I'd better not cross. Once, when I was twelve, after some neighbor girls complained about my BB gun, Mom and Dad told me to be more careful. Later, I took the gun and joined some friends down by a neighbor's pond. For a while I was content shooting at various inanimate objects in the water. But egged on by one of the other boys, I rolled five BBs into the barrel of the gun, then shot them all at once, like a shotgun, at a duck.

One BB hit the water about thirty feet out—and fifty feet short of the duck. Another hit the water at twenty feet, another at fifteen, another at thirteen, and the last one plopped into the pond at ten feet. I thought it was an intriguing experiment in kinetic energy.

My mother disagreed. When I came home, she met me halfway up our driveway, yanked the gun from my hands, and wrapped it around the trunk of the nearest black cherry tree. She ordered me to turn my bike around and head for the florist's shop, to pick up flowers for the lady who owned the pond. I was to deliver them in person and apologize for killing her duck. (One of the other boys had eventually shot it.) Although I hadn't come anywhere near to hitting it, in my mother's eyes I was guilty by association and by action. I was speechless before her passion for justice.

Delivering the flowers and apologizing for something I hadn't done was both awkward and humiliating, but it taught me never to cross a line my parents drew. Although Mom later said she had a strong feeling of compassion for me, and that she felt bad about trashing the gun, she never regretted doing it. I got the point and didn't make that mistake again. The line I crossed that day was like a solid wall that didn't move. It gave me a sense of security I wouldn't have had if my parents had been more lenient.

## Is This Overprotection?

When Dawson was eight, we once asked him to describe his favorite night. He said it's when we're all home and we read and do crafts together as a family. No videos, no Internet, no friends over, no television, no entertainment, no special treats—just family, stories, and creativity.

The song "Once Upon a Time" by Michael Martin Murphy echoes this sentiment:

> So turn the TV off,
> Put the video games away,
> Come sit down beside me,
> Tell me what you did today.[30]

How many nights like this do we experience? How many adults comprehend that this is what children desire, deep down in their hearts? Obviously this won't be very palatable for children who have already been captured by the competition. "Boring" would be the first word out of their mouths at the suggestion of the night Dawson described. But to him, a night like that, together, is great because it focuses on our relationship as a family.

Sometimes people have asked me: "Aren't you overprotecting your children?" To me, that question is illogical and fundamentally flawed. Of course I'm overprotecting my children! I would never think of underprotecting them, especially in a time when, as John Nieder expressed it, children's "young minds cannot comprehend information presented by an increasingly sick adult world."[31]

Our culture underprotects our children in the name of preparing them for adulthood—an idea that's fundamentally flawed. In their book *Saving Childhood,* Michael and Diane Medved say that preparation should mean learning such life skills as homemaking and family headship. By contrast, our secular society believes children should be prepared to live in a world permeated by violence, sex, and drugs. Children are exposed to these things at younger and younger ages so they can become "moral-dilemma literate." The world may believe this is necessary preparation for adulthood, but in reality all it's doing is shredding them and their innocence. Before puberty, children need to be children. Early destruction of innocence does them long-term damage and can cripple them with chronic psychological and spiritual problems as adults.[32]

There's a time for protection to decrease and preparation to increase, but only at appropriate age and developmental levels.

For Christian parents, the right kind of protection may mean closely monitoring their children's friends and extracurricular activities, controlling or throwing away the television, closely screening and limiting home videos, limiting Internet access, and eliminating unwholesome video games. For some it may require more radical steps such as simplifying their lifestyle, drastically modifying our vacation plans, considering educational alternatives such as home-schooling, or even moving to a new community.

## PUBLIC ENEMY NUMBER ONE

Protection from the harmful influence of TV and home videos is particularly crucial.

*In Endangered Minds: Why Our Children Don't Think—and What We Can Do About It,* Jane Healy also calls television "public enemy number one." She explores how TV artificially manipulates the brain into paying attention by violating its natural defense mechanisms with frequent visual and auditory changes; how it induces neural passivity and reduces "stick-to-itiveness"; how it may have a hypnotic and possibly neurologically addictive effect on the brain by changing the frequency of its electrical impulses in ways that block normal mental processing; and how it has all but displaced reading as a leisure activity.[33]

One moonlit summer night years ago, I went for a walk through a neighborhood in Tucson, Arizona. The perfume of blooming cacti and mesquite was in the air. All was peaceful and quiet. But something was wrong. The front porches were empty, and from every window came an eerie blue glow—light from television sets. The situation inspired me to write these lyrics: "Empty porches asked me, 'Where have all the children gone?' And from windows, unholy lights told of good deeds left undone." These words captured my sadness over television's impact on children when their parents are, as the song goes on to say, "in a daze."

Not only on TV but also in home videos, the amount of profanity—and particularly the taking of the Lord's name in vain—is much greater than most Christians realize. Many movies built around a great story, with positive characters and quality production, have questionable or even blasphemous language strategically sprinkled throughout, as though we were being subtly conditioned to accept it. We would never tolerate this from other sources. This sends a message to our children.

> *Heroic moments taken singly appear ordinary, but a lifetime of them is extraordinary.*

We may rationalize this away by thinking, *They'll have to face this someday, so why not let them face it in the safety of our home?* But surely this is counter to biblical thinking: "Finally, brethren, whatever things are true, whatever things are noble, whatever things are just, whatever things are pure, whatever things are lovely, whatever things are of good report, if there is any virtue and if there is anything praiseworthy—meditate on these things" (Philippians 4:8).

One simple, practical way to stop the barrage of crude words, profanity, and filth flowing from our video monitors is to purchase an electronic filter for the VCR or cable TV, which can be programmed for specific words to which Christian parents would never expose their children in other settings.

## TEAMWORK FOR PARENTS

As we parents walk the way of wisdom and invite our children to walk with us, the most important thing is that we walk together, always aware we have a divine companion walking with us and living in us.

For most of my childhood I lived in a one-story house my dad built. Every workday morning I heard my mother get up at a quarter to four. I remember the aroma of coffee drifting into the bedroom I shared with my brother. Mom packed my dad's lunch while breakfast was cooking. At four, she woke him and they talked together as they ate. Dad left for work in the predawn darkness, many times returning home after sundown, having worked ten or twelve hours through stifling heat and humidity or subzero cold. I often lay awake between the time Dad left and the time we were supposed to get up, wondering at my parents' strength to do this day after day. Their commitment, dedication, and willingness to sacrifice gave me a genuine sense of security.

My parents were a team, pressing on together toward the common goal of raising their sons. I believe it was their unconditional love, more than anything else, that won our hearts then and still binds us to them as adults. Their heroic moments taken singly appear ordinary, but a lifetime of them is extraordinary.

After many years of counseling young people, Jay Kesler, former president of Youth for Christ, observed that the only common thread he found among successfully raised children was that their parents hugged each other. Parents who aren't intimate friends, sharing the same goals for their family, don't ordinarily hug very much.

They also don't ordinarily pray together, which is one of the keys to developing and maintaining the intimacy in marriage that will draw children to Christ. Once when I was addressing a hundred Christian men, I asked, "How many of you regularly pray with your wife?" Three hands went up. It turned out that one man didn't understand the question and another was hedging. Only one out of a hundred did actually pray regularly with his wife.

Why so few? Some men have told me they find it difficult to move to an intimate relational level with their wife. It's emotionally awkward, so they avoid it. Beyond this, once a man has forced himself to do it and he's over the initial awkwardness, it's even harder for him to make it a daily discipline because of modern schedules and logistics.

One father told me he avoids praying with his wife because he's afraid the prayer will become a ritual and a moralistic platform for preaching to her. I think it's worth the risk. After all, we risk colliding with another vehicle every time we drive, but we still get behind the wheel.

A husband needs to catch the eternal vision and perspective of the Larger Story—the Sacred Romance—if he's to begin praying with his wife. Otherwise, it will be just a performance anyway. Sometimes it requires a shock to his life, such as being told his wife is terminally ill. Every man I've known who has been in that situation began earnestly praying both with and for his wife. Prayer infuses the power of God into any relationship, especially marriage.

## THE MOST IMPORTANT LOVE

Several years ago, our friend Vicky Goodchild told me, "The most important love we can give our children isn't the love we give them directly through our relationship with them, but the love we give them indirectly through the love we have for our spouse." With that idea in mind, she asked me to write a song about relationship. The chorus for the song goes like this:

> *And they'll know that we love them*
> *By the way that you love me,*
> *And the way that I love you*
> *Is what they want to see.*[34]

This is oneness demonstrated. A husband and wife loving each other provide security to their children and paint a living picture of Jesus Christ and His bride.

This doesn't mean single parents cannot successfully romance their child's heart. God's grace and power can enable a single parent to communicate the spiritual truths that underlie a marital relationship if he or she is in relational oneness with Christ. And God has promised that He is "father of the fatherless, a defender of widows" (Psalm 68:5). His special sustaining grace is extended to those who lack the equivalent human relationship.

I believe the body of Christ, expressed in the local church, is meant to provide Christian community through support groups and counseling/coaching. I believe it's strongly implied in Scripture that deacons are to minister to single parents.

A single-parent friend described it this way: "A father and

mother together see with two eyes—dimensionally, in stereo—while a single parent sees with only one eye." Depth of perception is more difficult, so it's important for a single parent to find godly mentors who can help bring a three-dimensional perspective into the life of their child. Two-parent families who open their homes to single-parent families give children without a father or a mother the opportunity to see and feel the oneness of a husband/wife relationship, which provides them a framework on which to hang their developing understanding of God's relationship with His children.

Oneness is foundational to romance. Parents living in true oneness, entering their child's world together, give authenticity to the message that they love their child with a true and good heart—as God does. Entering our child's world in the way Christ entered ours prepares the soil—and the soul—for the romance.

# Chapter 8

# Parental Incarnation

*So we traveled on back in my memories,*
*We got lost in boyhood dreams:*
*Baggy pants and a fishin' pole,*
*And carefree sunny days—*
*The child in me and my little boy*
*Became the best of friends.*

"DADDY, TAKE ME BACK"

When our friend Ray comes home from work, he enters the small world of each of his children. The second he walks in the door, he lays aside his adult power and positions himself on their level—first on his knees, then eventually lying on the floor with his kids climbing all over him. Then, even if only five minutes of daylight remain, he'll often grab a ball and take his kids outside to play. He knows that right now is really the only time he has available for his children.

To envision this properly, you need to know that Ray holds the record for tackles as a linebacker for the former national champion Colorado Buffaloes. Yet this big man has a passion for small things, from miniature cars to shadow boxes. His fingers are the biggest in the house, but he can untie the tiniest knot on his kids' sneakers.

As Ray wrestles or plays catch with his children, he continually shares facts and information he learns at work or in his reading. His older children are following his lead, sharing what they learn with the younger ones just as their dad does with them. As Ray and the kids watch a football game on television, they constantly discuss the finer points—offense, defense, the game plan, strategies, refereeing, and replays. In this way he redeems even the time spent watching an athletic event.

> *Our task is to so fully incarnate the character of God that our children will desire to follow Him.*

Ray told me once, "It's like giving up being an adult for a little while. And it's not easy. One reason I do this with my kids now is because I wish somebody had done it with me. But the biggest reason is that I want to have a close relationship with them—as close as possible—to win their hearts for Christ."

C. S. Lewis's Narnian logic would say that entering a child's world as an adult is hard because our adult world is actually the smaller world, constricted by adultish logic, limits, and concerns. The world of children is infinitely larger—its boundaries stretch to the limits of the imagination. It's filled with wonder, mystery, and adventure. Hope and optimism rule.

"And," says Ray, "when I'm in their world, the cares of mine go away for a while."

When Ray enters the world of his children he's following the example of Jesus, who entered our world to deliver God's message of love and to fulfill His plan of redemption—in person. "And the Word became flesh and dwelt among us.... No one has seen God at any time. The only begotten Son,

who is in the bosom of the Father, He has declared Him"
(John 1:14, 18).

## IF JESUS WERE A PARENT

Theologians call Jesus' taking on flesh "incarnation," from
the Latin words meaning "in flesh." The apostle Paul's celebration of Christ's choice reads like a hymn—which it is, in
the original Greek:

> Let this mind be in you which was also in Christ Jesus,
> who, being in the form of God, did not consider it
> robbery to be equal with God, but made Himself of no
> reputation, taking the form of a bondservant, and
> coming in the likeness of men. And being found in
> appearance as a man, He humbled Himself and
> became obedient to the point of death, even the death
> of the cross. (Philippians 2:5–8)

When parents lay aside their adultness to enter their
child's world, they incarnate the mind, or attitude, of the Lord
Jesus—our Servant-Savior, who romanced us to Himself by
demonstrating God's character. He said, "He who has seen Me
has seen the Father" (John 14:9). A primary purpose of Jesus'
life was to show us what God is like.

Our task as parents is similar—to so fully incarnate the
character of God that our children will desire to follow Him and
His way of wisdom. And His character is expressed in us through
the fruit of His Spirit: "Love, joy, peace, longsuffering, kindness,

goodness, faithfulness, gentleness, self-control" Galatians 5:22–23).
We cannot produce this spiritual fruit by trying harder. It comes
only by allowing the Spirit of God to live in and through us.

The apostle Paul exhorts us:

> Therefore be imitators of God as dear children. And
> walk in love, as Christ also has loved us and given
> Himself for us.... See then that you walk circumspectly,
> not as fools but as wise, redeeming the time, because
> the days are evil.... Understand what the will of the
> Lord is.... Be filled with the Spirit, submitting to one
> another in the fear of God. Wives, submit to your own
> husbands, as to the Lord. Husbands, love your wives,
> just as Christ also loved the church and gave Himself
> for her.... Children, obey your parents in the Lord, for
> this is right. And you, fathers, do not provoke your
> children to wrath, but bring them up in the training
> and admonition of the Lord. (Ephesians 5:1–2, 15–18,
> 21–22, 25; 6:1, 4)

I could have quoted only the last part about children, since
it seems to be the only portion relevant to our topic. But we
must understand this passage in its context to apply it properly
to parenting. The context is godly relationships as one journeys on the way of wisdom, and the basic attitude required is
the humility of a servant.

"Be imitators of God" is a clear command to parents.
What did God do that we should imitate? He, Jesus, accom-
plished our redemption by setting aside His divine rights and
power to become a human baby, born in a stable, worshiped

and adored by shepherds, wise men, a mother and an adoptive father, all of whom He, the Lord of the universe, had created. Even in that manger, Jesus was God incarnate. As He grew in stature and wisdom, and in favor with God and men, He remained God incarnate...still humbling Himself by remaining under the authority of Mary and Joseph, even though He, at the age of twelve, had been found in the temple, in the midst of the teachers, listening and asking questions.

He was tempted in every way we're tempted, but He did not sin. He had an itinerant ministry for about three years, healing, teaching, and discipling His chosen few until, unjustly condemned, He died a criminal's death on a Roman cross, demonstrating for time and eternity that God's omnipotent love conquers evil in all its forms.

I've heard a lot of men say they would gladly lay down their lives for their children. That's a laudable sentiment, but it's not often what their child perceives. Let's look at a child's side of the relationship:

One afternoon, as a father is editing the manuscript of his book on parenting, he hears the footsteps of his young son approaching his office door. He sighs. *Another interruption. I'll never finish this book!*

> *We romance our children by walking humbly before them and with them.*

Seconds later, still concentrating on his computer screen, he hears, "Dad, what is your consulting rate?"

The father says, "I'll tell you later. Can't you see I'm working?"

The son gets the message and obediently walks away.

Later that day the father is walking out the door for his

daily run when his son asks, "Dad, how much money do you make?"

"I'll discuss it with you later," he says. "I've got to exercise while it's still light."

"Okay," his son says, and goes off.

That evening after dinner, the father has just settled into the couch with a book he needs to read as background for his manuscript when his son approaches him again. "Dad, how much do you charge your clients?"

This time the father is annoyed. He has put in a long day. He's tired and ready to relax with his book before going to bed. Besides, he's about to read the chapter on how to be a better father—so this is a legitimate activity. He says, "Give me a few minutes and I'll come up to your room and discuss it with you."

An hour and a half later, the father walks into his son's dark room. His child's even breathing tells him the boy is sound asleep. In the dim light the father can see that on the table next to his bed is an overturned piggy bank. All his son's money has been sorted into piles. On a piece of paper in columns his boy has added up pennies, nickels, dimes, and quarters. Written at the bottom of the paper are the words, "I hope this will be enough to buy an hour with Dad."

Although this story is fictitious, I can be as guilty as other Christian fathers of wasting opportunities to be with my son when he simply expresses an interest, needs my companionship, and desires to share his heart and be my friend. To squander these moments is a loss that will someday grieve and break our hearts, when the footsteps are no longer heard at our office doors. The challenge is to seize every moment, every day. This is what the apostle Paul means when he says that wise people redeem, or make the most of, their time.

The key to understanding and applying the core message of Ephesians 5 and 6 to parenting is the phrase "the training [nurture] and admonition [instruction] of the Lord." In other words, we can be successful as parents only as we learn to emulate the sacrificial love of Jesus Christ in our relationship with our children.

We romance our children by walking humbly before them and with them. When they see and experience the superiority of the way of wisdom, it dazzles them, woos them, and draws them, captivating them like the best story they've ever heard.

Jesus became one of us so He could communicate with us, know us, identify with us—with our joys and sorrows, our testings, tears, pain, even separation for a time from those He loved. If we're to imitate Him and win the hearts of our children to Him, we must realize that gaining or exercising power is not the central issue.

We cannot control our children's watershed choice by controlling what they eat or wear, their choice of music or hairstyle, what sports or hobbies they pursue, their friendships, or other exposure to the youth subculture. Although it's necessary and appropriate to protect our children during childhood, parental power of this type is feeble compared to the power of love. Compliance is not the goal of Christlike parenting. "Perfect" behavior—whatever that is—can be enforced for a time, but eventually every child will emerge from the parents' control.

Children whose spirits have been beaten down for years, through forced compliance in the name of Christianity, often bear the fruit of rebellion. Through their overzealous control the parents have exasperated their children, provoking them to wrath and producing the opposite result of what they'd hoped for.

Force may achieve certain short-term goals, including making the parents look good to their peers. But force will never win a heart. Only sacrificial love can do that. Power may control conduct for a time, but only romance can produce sincere love. At the core of romance is our credibility as fellow pilgrims, with our children, on the journey we call life. We're either on this journey together or separately, and they know this—at first intuitively, then by observation as they mature.

> *The son's worst fear wasn't a spanking, but hearing the words "You've disappointed me."*

Just as Jesus stepped down from His throne to share our journey, we must step down from the self-importance of our adult world to communicate and connect with our children. We must view their decisions and behavior in the context of their lives, not ours. Jesus was still God when He walked among us, and we'll still be adults when we enter our children's world. But both incarnations have the same goal—connecting on the level of the heart for the purpose of redemption.

Our pastor once related how he and some friends found a copy of *Playboy* in a field, when he was seven. The future pastor knew pornography was something his father hated, both for what it represented and for what it might do to his son. But the temptation proved too powerful, and he and his friends amazed themselves with what they saw in the magazine—a beautiful thing twisted and corrupted by the other suitor.

The boy had planned to keep the incident secret, but within hours of returning home he could no longer keep it to himself. He called his father into his room where, through a flood of tears, shaking and sobbing, he confessed his sin. Instead of receiving the belt, he received from his father a hug, and this assurance: "Peter, I forgive you." And then, because the father saw that the punishment his son was inflicting on himself was worse than a thousand spankings, he gently inquired, as he left the room, "Are you going to be okay?"

The key to this interchange wasn't just what happened in those few minutes, but what had taken place during the previous seven years. All the boy's life his father had disciplined him, but he had shepherded him, too. The son's worst fear wasn't a spanking, but hearing the words "You've disappointed me." The father's love had earned a higher place of authority in the son's heart than any paddle could occupy.

This parallels the Christian's deepest concern—that they might grieve the Holy Spirit. Through the years, our pastor's father had not just told him what keys to punch on the piano of life, but he'd let the boy hear the music of his parents' incarnational love.

Parental love like this always takes sacrifice. There's no other way.

I recall an incident involving our son Travis that occurred when he was five years old. I can still see him standing on the porch outside our sliding glass door that spring day, as Karey described his misbehavior—the nature of which none of us can remember now. But we all remember what happened next. It was my duty to administer the proper justice. But when I looked at our little boy, so sorry and scared and obviously willing to accept any punishment I decreed, the traditional discipline just didn't seem right. The next thing that happened surprised even me. "Travis," I said, "I'll take the spanking for you."

Karey administered it with surprising severity as Travis watched in horror. Through the creativity that only God's Spirit could have provided at that moment, God used me and a paddle as His means to incarnate for Travis the meaning of grace and the sacrificial love of Jesus. It so impressed Travis that he never again needed a spanking. In fact, I can't recall his ever being defiant or rebellious again.

There's a place for spankings or groundings, suspensions of privileges, or whatever methods of discipline may work best with each of our children. But whatever means we employ should always serve the larger goal of romance, with a view toward winning a lifelong place of authority and influence in our child's heart.

For the sake of love, Jesus became like us. He sent the Holy Spirit to live in all believers so we can become like Him. Where the Spirit of the Lord is, there is liberty—not license and not fear, but freedom to be all He called us to be. If we become like our children, they'll want to become like us. And the romance we offer will empower them to do so.

Such servant love is sacrificial, exhausting, and sometimes messy, for the child controls the time and energy required. It's humbling, for example, when we have to say, "I'm sorry." It's courageous, for it takes great courage to lay aside parental power, knowing we cannot control the outcome, which may include pain when the child makes mistakes.

By contrast, grasping parental power and refusing to take the risks seems safer. We may feel more secure when we keep our children dependent on us, emotionally and financially, imposing our will through bribery or threats. It seems to reduce our vulnerability when we always rescue them, instead of giving them the freedom to fail. Control and dignity seem more assured if we hold tight to the reins.

But children can sometimes pretend even better than adults. Thus it's possible to reform behavior without changing the heart, and compliance without heart is deadly to the development of authentic faith. The parent may seem to win in the short term, but the coerced child, apart from God's grace, is most likely to become a rebel or a pharisee, whose soul will eventually shrivel up and die. George MacDonald put it bluntly:

> *Compliance without heart is deadly to the development of authentic faith.*

But the more familiar one becomes with any religious system while yet the conscience and will are unawakened and obedience has not begun, the harder is it to enter into the kingdom of heaven. Such familiarity is a soul-killing experience, and great will be the excuse for some of those sons of religious parents who have gone further towards hell than may be born and bred thieves and sinners.[35]

Sinful behavior obviously originates in a sinful heart, but doctrinally correct behavior can also originate in a sinful heart. All of us have sinful hearts because of our sin nature, but through Christ our hearts can be made new. Is our child's relationship with Him dynamic and growing, or stale and stagnant? Is it a relationship of deep, romantic love or a relationship with ideas, concepts, words, and works? If the latter, the child will almost surely fall, for the other suitor of the soul will find a way to convince him that sinning "just this once" isn't such a big deal. But if the child's relationship with Christ is deep and strong, the Savior will whisper, "I am yours, and you are Mine. We'll stand against this trickery together."

## SEEING GOD IN STEREO

I believe it's most important that the father be the romance leader in the home. Remember the apostle's exhortation to fathers: not to exasperate their children but to bring them up in the training and instruction of the Lord.

One summer I mentored an eighteen-year-old boy. It was a transitional time for "Joe." He'd been depressed for several years, partly because of his parents' divorce. During the school year he'd been living in a semi-lockdown Christian boarding school—a place for youth who were beyond the help of their parents. I thought if Joe lived with us for the summer, I might be able to reach past the hurt to his heart.

One thing I neglected to factor in was how Karey's pattern of relating to Joe might differ from mine. I was so focused on winning his heart that I sometimes looked past his behavior, though I drew the line at anything I felt might negatively affect our family. Karey was so focused on his behavior that she found it impossible to form a personal relationship with Joe. Looking back, I think this unresolved tension taught both Karey and me a lesson—we gravitated to two different approaches. In spite of our differences, we did win his heart, though he continued to struggle with his behavior. Bad habits, addictions, and lack of self-control are much harder to change once a child is grown.

I suspect that what Karey and I experienced that summer might be common. Mothers and fathers have differing roles in the romance. I believe the most common pattern is for the husband to focus on principles—the big picture or the goal— while the wife tends to focus on down-to-earth details.

Once Karey spent two weeks in the hospital, and I was the homemaker. As most men know, the job is impossible—for us. Women really do seem to have eyes in the backs of their heads. They're aware of who's playing where, who's fighting, what glass is breaking, what's being flushed down the toilet, and who's swallowing what. At the same time, they're putting a meal on the table.

Women typically have 40 percent more connection than men between the left and right lobes of the brain. While a male baby is in the womb, sex-related hormones and chemicals destroy some of the connecting corpus callosum between the two lobes. Girls enter the world with more two-sided thinking than boys. Messages and electrical impulses travel faster between the two lobes. This in a sense specializes the brains of men and women into two different ways of thinking.

The left brain houses more of the logical, analytical, factual, and aggressive centers of thought, while the right lobe houses feelings, relationship, language, and communication skills. It's said that women comprehend more information than men do as they walk into a room. This is because a man tends to focus on the destination, which in this case may be a person in the room, whereas women are more conscious of the details along the way.

This difference is often reflected in the way a mother and father romance their child's heart. Although romance may be more important to women, men are traditionally the initiators—knights in shining armor, with more of a proactive role.

Often it's hard to judge, in the raising of a child, which spouse has better balance in focusing on behavior or romance, especially as the child's needs change according to age and personality. Perhaps the husband and wife together create the ideal balance. We at least are wise to acknowledge that such differences exist, thus avoiding confusion and conflict that can only hinder our achievement of the ultimate goal.

A story told by our pastor illustrates this well: Tom and Jane have a three-year-old son, Brandon. One day Tom comes home from work, too exhausted to do anything but sit on the love seat in front of the TV, his arm around Jane. Brandon, on the other hand, has lots of energy. He runs into the dining room, grabs a chair, and drags it to the kitchen—scratching the floor along the way. He climbs onto the counter and opens the cupboard. As he takes out a cup, several fall to the floor. On his way down, Brandon grabs a bag of cookies, but it snags and rips, scattering cookies everywhere. Jane is about to intervene, but Tom gently restrains her because he wants to see what their minicyclone will do next.

Brandon is already at the refrigerator. He pulls out a gallon jug of milk, but it is too heavy and he drops it. The lid pops off, and suddenly the kitchen floor is swimming in a cookie milk shake.

Next, just as Tom is about to exert his authority to protect his home, Brandon picks a cup out of the mess, pours in some milk, scrapes up some cookie remains from the floor onto a plate, and runs toward his father, saying, "Daddy, I made it for you!"

Unfortunately, the little boy's foot catches on the carpet right in front of his parents. Brandon does a face plant in Daddy's lap at just about the time the cookies and milk arrive.

What do the parents see? Jane sees an awful mess and a child who needs training. Tom sees a son who loves him enough to bring him cookies and milk when he's tired.

Yes, they'll clean up the floor together. Yes, they'll work on Brandon's kitchen skills. But first they'll enjoy this rare moment together. Having a clean kitchen is nowhere near as important as reinforcing the love that made it dirty. In this, Tom and Jane are incarnating the love of God for Brandon—and for them—a love that ignores the pervasive messiness of our lives in favor of the beauty of a heart in love with Him. Such a heart is produced not by power but by romance, a big-picture process focused on what's happening in a child's heart.

## THE KEYSTONE OF A CHILD'S HEART

Traditionally, the words training, discipling, and mentoring have been used to describe various approaches to winning a child's heart. More recently, shepherding has come into use through a book by Tedd Tripp. These words actually describe different kinds of relationships common between parents and children. They seem to overlap in practice, but there are significant differences.

Training is essentially the development of habits. The key

parenting concept is molding the will without breaking the spirit. This goal is especially important for young children, not only for their character development but also for their safety and well-being. Training also instills skills and behavior essential for living in society. An untrained child will usually have difficulty controlling his behavior even after his heart has been won.

Discipling is teaching spiritual truths and/or academic knowledge. The goal is mastery of spiritual disciplines and acquisition of knowledge through a course of study that lasts for a lim-ited time. Discipling is driven by the discipler's agenda; respect for the discipler is required. A person may disciple hundreds of individuals during his or her lifetime. Today it's common for the discipler to follow a manual written by a more experienced and mature discipler. It's typically adminis-trated through a local church program, or a discipling-focused parachurch organization.

> *Romance is the keystone in the arch that represents a child's spiritual structure.*

Mentoring is caring for, helping, and supporting a person toward maturity—in essence, it's the development of a person. It's practical exposure to all relevant areas of life, and it is more relationship-focused than content-focused. It concerns the protégé's goals and agenda. It's usually a long-term commit-ment and process that doesn't require a specific curriculum. Respect and a natural compatibility or attraction are necessary. Mentoring is done most naturally between a parent and a child, but other relationships are also common and effective. A person may mentor many individuals during a lifetime. Jesus Christ mentored twelve.

Shepherding is the blending of discipling and mentoring in the context of parenting. It balances behavior training with heart training, showing a child how to know God and the true nature of reality. It infects children with a worldview that's focused on glorifying God and enjoying Him forever. Shepherding leads a child on a path of discovery, discernment, and wisdom.

In summary, training deals with the development of proper behavior and good habits; discipling emphasizes knowledge and disciplines; mentoring emphasizes the application of these to life; while shepherding includes them all with a focus on changing the heart, not just the behavior.

These approaches are foundational to the winning of a child's heart, but they're of little value if the child doesn't develop a heart after God. This happens through romance, which we can picture as the keystone in the top of an arch that represents a child's spiritual structure (see keystone arch illustration at the end of this chapter). Without this keystone, the arch will collapse, for the wedge-shaped keystone locks the other pieces in place, making a strong and stable structure. Of course, without the other pieces in place, there's no place in which to set the keystone. A heart that's won without spiritual training, discipline, biblical knowledge, and wisdom will flounder. It will be carried away, irresponsible and foolish, in the currents of culture.

While I was writing this chapter, Dawson spent two full days designing and building with LEGOs. He was an engineer, architect, and sculptor. The whole dining room table was covered with his creations—Native American villages, forts, cities, skyscrapers, animals.

The third morning, as I was researching arches, vaults, and keystones, I heard Dawson waking up. Before he came downstairs, I ran over to his creations, got down on my knees and started playing with them. As he came into the room, I didn't even have to see the smile on his face as he walked up behind me—I could feel it. I had demonstrated how I valued his work, his art. He saw the child alive in me. This deepened our relationship as I shared in his passion and accomplishment. He knew where my affections lay, because I'd taken the time and invested the energy to enter and share his world with him.

Parental incarnation really isn't that hard, after all.

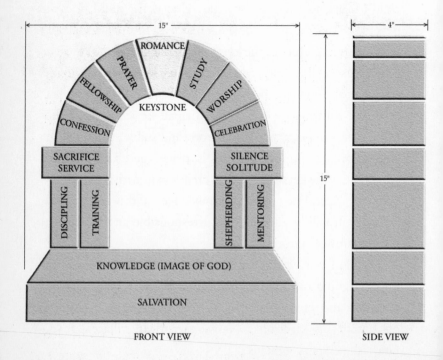

FRONT VIEW                    SIDE VIEW

Chapter 9

# Profile of a Romancer

*I've heard that they are angels in disguise,*
*If you want to find a treasure, just look into their eyes.*
*And the touch of tiny fingers will make the foolish wise,*
*So watch for these angels in disguise.*

"ANGELS IN DISGUISE"

As we enter our child's world, we're faced with a daunting reality. How do we connect? How do we relate? What should characterize our relationship?

In Ephesians 5:2 we find a partial answer in the phrase "sweet-smelling aroma." Apostle Paul says that this is what we should be. Something sweet is attractive, pleasant, and desired, and aroma refers to a distinctive quality that emanates from within—not cheap perfume but the authentic "essence" of romance.

## A CHILDLIKE HEART

Our church hosts a costume party called Family Fun Night as an alternative to Halloween. Several years ago, three nights before, Heather and Travis reminded me they needed costumes. That year's theme was biblical characters.

Impulsively, I suggested Jonah and the whale. Karey got question marks in her eyes, so I said, "Heather will be the whale. Travis will be Jonah. And I will be the designer and builder—the creator."

> *Can we afford not to be childlike if we want to romance our children's hearts?*

We spent the next three days sculpting the whale from cardboard, papier-mâché, and wood, then painted it blue. It was thirteen feet long, five feet tall—and three feet wide, so we could still squeeze it through our front door. It had a hinged tail that moved back and forth, controlled by a stick inside. The front half had no bottom, so Heather and Travis could propel it by holding onto a waist-high pole inside, and walking. When Heather lifted the pole, the whale's head rose and the mouth opened wide— I hinged it so the lower jaw would rest on the floor by gravity. White teeth lined the opening.

We'd read somewhere that Jonah got the attention of the people of Nineveh because he was bleached white by the stomach acids of the whale. So we bleached Travis's clothes and painted him white. We attached a lobster and seaweed to his shoulder. When he stepped out of the whale's mouth, like the original Jonah, he caught everyone's attention. As I recall, they didn't even take a vote—our costume was, fins down, the best by far. But that didn't matter. What mattered was that Travis and Heather had been on a wild, three-day ride with Mr. Dad, whose childlike imagination had been unleashed.

C. S. Lewis said, "When I became a man I put away childish things, including the fear of childishness and the desire to be very grown up."[36] But wait! Isn't that an oxymoron—a mature man with a childlike heart? A childlike heart produces irresponsible, frivolous behavior. A child's nonverbal vocabulary includes skipping, hopping, dancing, jumping, running, laughter, peekaboos and winks.

Can a parent—particularly a father—afford the luxury of a childlike heart? A better question is, can we afford not to be childlike if we want to romance our children's hearts?

I once heard of a father who planned a wonderful vacation for his family. He was always dependable, but this time, at the last minute, he told them something had come up at the office and he wouldn't be able to go. He assured them they would have a great time without him. So the mother and kids packed their suitcases and drove off.

Meanwhile, the father flew to a city he knew they would be driving through, and the next time they saw him he was standing along the interstate with his thumb out! Imagine the scene as the children saw their father, hitchhiking. Extravagant? Perhaps. But our children are gifts from God Himself. No price is too great when we're trying to win their hearts.

Teddy Roosevelt was my grandfather's hero, so I've heard many stories about this great man. In his biographies I've always been struck by the descriptions of his relationship with his children. Tender, true, and winsome, he was their playmate, whether racing or roughhousing. He put as much energy into an obstacle race on the White House lawn as he did in a presidential campaign. He was both champion for and champion of his family, helping them grow in courage, strength, and compassion, inspiring them to ever-richer adventure and higher service—with him leading the way.

Once, the president was entertaining visiting statesmen

when he exclaimed, "I must ask you to excuse me. We'll finish this talk some other time. I promised the boys I'd go shooting with them at four o'clock, and I never keep boys waiting. It's a hard trial for a boy to wait." This man knew how to romance his children's hearts.

Roosevelt also gave his heart to his children, through his actions and his pen. He wrote thousands of letters to them. I suspect many fathers today haven't written even one letter to their children.

> We must remember how to play.

I know when I receive a letter or package, the handwritten part always captures my attention first. My sister-in-law, Linda, believes there's something special about handwritten letters—they communicate the heart in a way e-mails or telephone conversations cannot. She loves to write notes to her children, and they save them—even hang them on their walls. But she also sends nonverbal "notes" in the best of an endearing, childlike spirit. Her children shared with me how, besides enclosing little jokes and notes in their lunches, she often takes a bite out of each of their sandwiches—just to remind them how much she loves them. When they open their lunch boxes they all say, "Oh, Mom!" because there, for their friends to see, is her "love bite."

To enter God's kingdom, Jesus said, we must receive it as a little child. We must take it simply as a gift—coming not because we deserve it, but by grace. He gave His disciples a classic lesson when they argued about who should be the greatest in the kingdom. Jesus set a little child before them, to show them the true nature of the kingdom. In Mark 9–10 and Matthew 18 He told them they couldn't enter into the kingdom except by becoming like little children—by humbling themselves. This is an infinite truth because it provides insight into the fundamental nature of God.

When children throw themselves creatively, imaginatively, and wholeheartedly into whatever they're doing, they're unself-conscious in the most basic sense—forgetting about themselves. The Greek word for ultimate self-consciousness is hubris, which means "pride"—us as the center of the universe. The childlikeness Jesus spoke of is the opposite—to be hopelessly enthralled, responsive, and open to the possibility that fairy tales are true after all—that there really is a "place beyond time"—a "Brigadoon." Childlikeness resurrects heartfelt visions of our true home and our heavenly Father.

We need to find a way to nurture and nourish the child within us before we can hope to romance the hearts of our children. There's no formula or checklist, no "ten steps to recovery" program. We must simply set the inner child free again. We must remember how to play.

If we become playmates to our children, we'll be half the way back home.

## EVERYDAY HERO

My father, eighty years old as I write this, is still a hero to me. The image of God's fatherhood still flows out of his life, an image not of sophisticated theology or great religious works but of genuine trust and relationship with God.

Our family never missed church. There was no question about that. One Sunday, my dad drove us there through a blinding blizzard. In Wisconsin, that means something you might expect just south of the North Pole—snow falling horizontally at sixty miles an hour, wind howling through tightly shut doors and windows. You know if you get stuck on the road they'll find your frozen body in the spring, after the drifts have receded to twelve feet high.

We could barely see the hood of the car. The ice built up so fast the windshield wipers looked like PVC pipes. Not even suicidal snowmobilers were out. How we made it I'll never understand, but we did—to discover we were the only ones there. The preacher hadn't even made it—and the parsonage was next door! That we got there and back left an indelible impression on me.

*All of us—especially our children—yearn for a real Superman.*

I also watched my father sit at the dining room table, a few minutes before we left for church, to write the family's weekly tithe check. Even as a youth, I perceived this as a serious, hallowed moment. It told me in no uncertain terms where my parents' treasures were.

Dad gave freely, sacrificially, of everything he had. And he loved me with no strings attached—my agenda was his.

When I began building my first home, he was there laying out the construction, sawing, and pounding nails. Many times now, when I call home, Mom will say, "Dad is out in the pole barn." Then she describes his passionate reaction to some challenging problem. You can tell she loves him and stands in awe of the optimism bubbling out of his boyish heart.

Recently I found in our attic a cedar box Dad built years ago, just so he could send a Big Wheel to Travis as a Christmas gift. In my eyes, the box reflected his resourcefulness, since he used what he had at the time to accomplish his goal. One year, for Heather's birthday, I rebuilt that box by lining it with aromatic cedar and adding brass hardware. I left the distressed look on the outside. Now it's a beautiful chest that Heather will have as a keepsake to remind her of her grandfather.

Dad had trouble swallowing in the fall of 2000, and was soon diagnosed with an aggressive form of esophageal cancer. This took our family completely by surprise. Fortunately, Mom and Dad live near a world-class medical center specializing in research, so he was soon assigned to a team of top-notch physicians.

The doctors did all the tests and decided to make Dad a project. They said he had the body of a much younger man, making him a great candidate for aggressive treatment, but they were stunned even more by his simple, strong, childlike faith. Why did "simple" and "childlike" impress these highly educated physicians? Because God's Spirit was obviously present. In fact, the doctors refused to give a formal prognosis; they couldn't quantify his chances. This of course left us all up in the air—right where we should have been, anyway, resting in God.

Dad began radiation and chemotherapy immediately, and he did well, just as the doctors predicted. One tense moment came at the height of the treatment when he decided to go deer hunting. He parked his four-wheeler and walked a short distance to his tree stand, but was too weak to climb the tree, so he sat at its base until dark. Then he returned to the four-wheeler, but it wouldn't start, and he was too weak even to begin walking down the logging road back home.

He would have frozen to death, except that a guardian

angel in the form of a neighbor walked out of the woods and helped him home. Apparently he'd been watching over Dad the whole time. Later, his primary care doctor said, "It's important during treatment to continue your normal routine—although this is beyond what I would call normal."

The radiation and chemo killed the cancer. Dad had the affected part of his esophagus removed through major surgery, and he returned to normal. During one of his last checkups, my mother thanked the physician in charge and remarked how wonderful the clinic was—the personnel, the choice of treatment, and of course the fact that many people were praying. The doctor looked her in the eye and said, "Ma'am, I would reverse the order if I were you."

My mother recovered quickly from the horrible shock of the initial diagnosis. Through the long ordeal, she courageously supported Dad—never losing hope. She told me God is the only explanation for the strength she found. Watching her face this overwhelming challenge inspired all of us, and drew us closer to God.

Travis once played a song for me, performed by a band with the curious name "Crash Test Dummies." The message has haunted me ever since. The chorus goes like this:

> Superman never made any money
> For savin' the world from Solomon Grundy
> And sometimes I despair the world will never see
> Another man like him.[37]

The message of the song is elusive and subtle. When I asked Travis what he thought, he said it gave him an overwhelming feeling of nostalgic sadness. I believe the last two lines sum up the point. All of us—especially our children—yearn for a real Superman. The longing ripples through our dreams. We've experienced it through many of the tragic figures in history, who were deprived of this image.[38]

Parents are heroes and heroines, larger than life, in their children's eyes. These natural and important roles give children a vision of what they wish to be. Children develop goals and a higher purpose for their lives, as they lift their gaze from the ground to the stars, toward God rather than man.

> *Joy amid adversity is one of the surest signs we're consciously living within a Larger Story.*

Mothers and fathers complement each other in these roles. A father may portray the brave-hearted image of God the Father, protecting us and taking us on great adventures; a mother may represent the tender, kind-hearted mercy of Christ, who reached out and touched us with unconditional sacrificial love. These images emanate not so much from the actions as from the hearts of mothers and fathers, and color forever their children's perceptions of God.

## COURAGEOUS SPIRIT

Recently, I had a once-in-a-lifetime spiritual experience as I said good-bye to a great man, Colonel Dick Kail. He was a mentor and spiritual elder in my life for years.

Dick had a powerful ministry to couples in the military. He'd lived his own life well, from Vietnam to the Pentagon.

The last time I visited with him, most of his household was in boxes, as he and his wife Brenda were moving back East. Dick was wearing a plastic body brace because his backbone was crumbling. After a seven-year battle with cancer, he was nearing the end of his earthly life.

This kind of visit can be heart-wrenching and depressing, but Dick's courage and spirit were inspirational. As he sat on the lone couch left in the house, Dick encouraged me as I've never been encouraged before. He gave me a fresh, eternal perspective for life that brought the Sacred Romance into clear focus.

As always, Dick wanted to know what I'd been doing. I told him about my investment of time and resources into the lives of families who sincerely desire to live biblically, and described the concept of romancing a child's heart. I mentioned this book and how I hoped it would help.

Dick then asked if I'd seen the movie *Saving Private Ryan*. I told him I thought it would be too graphic, and also that I felt I already had a deep appreciation for the horror and the cost of war. My grandfather had fought in the First World War, and the stories he told me were filled with passion and sacrifice.

Dick's view was that people who are ignorant of what it cost to win their freedom would benefit by seeing *Saving Private Ryan*. "The movie is accurate—almost too accurate," he agreed, "with bodies of fallen soldiers everywhere on the D-day beaches, body parts tossing in the surf, wounded soldiers limping and barely crawling while snipers systematically take them out.

"That depiction of war," Dick continued, "is a realistic

picture of spiritual warfare. Your ministry, in the same way, is a matter of life and death. In your neighborhood there are many mothers and fathers who have lost heart—whose souls are wounded. Many are captives in prisons of despair, addiction, and boredom. We were born into this war. It has been long and vicious and all around us parents are taking hits and collapsing.

"Monte," he said, and his eyes looked deeply into mine, "I see things very clearly. The vision you just shared with me of winning children's hearts, of the biblical balance you seek between supporting your family, following your calling, and engaging in ministry, is right on track. Don't be distracted by other voices. Listen to your heart and to God's Spirit. Live this script you shared with me, because God is obviously the Author of it. I feel it, sense it, and know it."

Then, with all the strength he could muster, he stood up, gave me a hug, and said, "I'll be seeing you in heaven."

The power in Dick's words was intensified by the heat of the crucible from which God was about to remove him. His own pain acted like a prism to focus, clarify, and beautify the "last words" of this great man. Later that day, I shared the experience with my son Travis, who was deeply moved because he knew Dick and sensed in my spirit the sacredness of this story.

William Gurnall said that hell is enraged by the image of God reflected in His children. Against this, he added, "demons hurl their mightiest weapons." Those moments I spent with Dick were a witness to the image of Christ in him, and the reality of the Larger Story—more evidence for Travis that hope for a Christian extends beyond life on earth.

## JOYFUL HEART

Our ability to experience joy in the midst of adversity is one of the surest signs we're consciously living within a Larger Story. When the last page is turned, we know the chapter including our present suffering will be but a vague memory. Children who see this in their parents will be drawn—romanced—to the Source of their parents' hope, as Travis and I were drawn to the Source of Dick's hope. And they'll be far more likely to adopt the same perspective when sorrow comes to them.

Our witness to our children as we share times of distress can either confuse them or connect them to Christ, who has promised there'll be no more death or crying or pain when the old order of things has passed away (Revelation 21:1–5).

There will be only joy in His new world. When we have this joy now—especially in the face of great difficulty—it confirms to our children that we really do believe in something bigger, more beautiful, more wonderful than life itself. This is real evidence of a firsthand relationship with almighty God.

C. S. Lewis knew deep sorrow and joy. In his book *A Grief Observed,* we find the "mad midnight moments" of a husband watching his wife, Joy, slowly die of cancer. In his earlier autobiographical book, *Surprised by Joy,* we find the meanderings of a skeptic who flees the hound of heaven through the labyrinth of his own mind until he returns to the faith of his youth, but with a more mature perspective. He describes the Spirit's invitation to faith as "like distant music which you need not listen to unless you wish, like a delicious faint wind on your face which you can easily ignore…. The odd thing is that something inside me suggested that it would be 'sensible' to refuse the invitation.... Then I silenced the inward wiseacre. I accepted the invitation...and passed in a state, which can be described only as joy."[39]

In *The Screwtape Letters,* Lewis plays a literal "devil's advocate" through the incisive and increasingly vitriolic letters of Screwtape to his understudy, Wormwood. As I read these letters, I can almost hear Lewis laughing in the background. Such levity disgusts devils, according to Screwtape, because it suggests a larger reality—which the devils cannot comprehend—the deep joy of knowing that what we see with our physical eyes is passing away, while what is seen by the eyes of the heart is eternal (2 Corinthians 4–5). Screwtape writes:

> Among adults some pretext in the way of jokes is usually provided, but the facility with which the smallest witticisms produce laughter at such a time shows that they are not the real cause. What the real cause is we do not know.... Laughter of this kind does us no good and should always be discouraged. Besides, this phenomenon is of itself disgusting and a direct insult to the realism, dignity, and austerity of hell.[40]

Jesus promised His disciples that His joy would be in them and their joy would be complete (John 15:11, NIV). Joy-induced laughter makes perfect sense for a Christian, though many seem to be about as oriented to "realism, dignity, and austerity" as the devils of hell. At the heart of Christianity is joy. It's a gigantic secret that draws us, woos us, and romances us into the company of the cross, which Jesus endured "for the joy set before him" (Hebrews 12:2, NIV)—our redemption.

The journey for us can be long, difficult, and exhausting, but when we least expect it, when our hope is nearly extinguished, a turn or a twist can surprise us and produce a knowing smile and, soon, laughter. It's an inside joke between us and the One writing the script of the Larger Story, the last mile along the country road of our childhood before reaching Grandma's house for Thanksgiving dinner after a thousand-mile trip.

In those willing to live in it, the reality of the Sacred Romance produces C. S. Lewis's nostalgic longing for heaven: "The feeling that you are coming back tho' to a place you have never yet reached."[41] Lewis also said, "Our best havings are wantings."[42] Proverbs 25:25 reminds us: "As cold water to a weary soul, so is good news from a far country."

The best news from a distant land is really a reminder that we're just pilgrims now, on the way to an eternal destination sometimes called heaven but known today as Joy.

## HEART OF LAUGHTER

If you're like me, you're far more attracted to someone who can laugh than to someone as serious as death all the time. We're drawn to this type of Christian because they seem to have a special, personal, and intimate connection with God. One of my friends makes me laugh, but sometimes after the fact I can't recall what was so funny. We were out to dinner once and he kept us laughing for nearly two hours, until I started getting cheek cramps. The strange thing was, afterwards I couldn't recall a single joke. It was more a sense of lightheartedness, marked by wit, that made our night so enjoy-able. Plus, knowing that this particular person had all the reason in the world to be bitter instead.

A joyous heart—especially in someone who could as easily be sad—is a testimony to the redeeming power of God and an affront to Satan. We all have one reason or another to be sad. Humor, gladness, a childlike heart—these are "a direct insult to the realism, dignity, and austerity of hell" because the devil wants humans to believe that the hopelessness of sorrow renders everything, even life itself, futile.

> *A joyous heart is an affront to Satan.*

Chuck Bolte once told me, "Fear and laughter are close bedfellows; which of the two will be experienced is deter-mined by the direction the story twists or turns in the end. The pleasure we derive in laughing is an enjoyment of relief from a negative or perplexing expectation."

Bob Farewell and I were discussing this very point by phone as he watched Hurricane Floyd barely miss their Florida home. "Humor," he said, with relief in his voice, "is the purging of tension."

The medical profession has recently rediscovered that humor is good medicine. In this, they echo Solomon: "A merry heart does good, like medicine" (Proverbs 17:22). Laughter has the power to disarm an adversary, open a closed spirit, and even stimulate a person's immune system.

It's common to overlook laughter in the romance of our children's hearts, because it seems so familiar, so ordinary—even earthy. It's easy to lose our ability to laugh as we work hard meeting the responsibilities of parenting. But if we're in relationship with God, we'll fit the same description that someone once gave C. S. Lewis—having "a sunny heart...and ready to burgeon out at any moment" with gladness.[43]

Few children will trust a father who rarely laughs, for his heart is a mystery. One of a father's most endearing qualities is the ability to laugh at himself—in front of his children.

Sometimes we have no choice. One day, I turned on our tap and filled a new dark blue enamel cup with ice-cold mountain water from our well. I took a sip and thought it tasted funny. Looking into the cup, I saw an oil slick on the surface. I dumped it out and filled it again. Another sip, another oil slick, swirling with rainbow colors.

Immediately, I alerted Karey and instructed the family not to drink our water, because it was contaminated with oil. With our children watching, I, their heroic protector, launched my investigation.

> *Humor opens up our children's hearts.*

This was right up my alley. I threw all my training and experience in engineering and geology at the problem. I racked my brain to come up with possible sources for the oil. I called several friends who were water-system experts. I consulted well water companies from the phone book. I had long technical conversations. I felt like the Sherlock Holmes of home water pollution.

The only conclusion I could draw was that the pump deep in our well had begun to leak oil.

After several days of drinking bottled water, I examined the oil slicks with my geologic hand lens, and noticed tiny white particles floating in the oil. These, I suspected, were chemical precipitates. I immediately reported this to my expert friends, who were even more mystified.

Then, quite by accident, I examined a glass of bottled water from which I'd taken a drink. It, too, contained oil! This confused me. Then I filled a glass from our tap and examined it. No oil. Then it dawned on me that the oil slicks appeared only after I'd taken a sip of the water. The "oil," it turned out, was from my own lip balm! We all wear lip protection in Colorado at dry times of the year. I'd never seen it before because I'd never drunk our well water from a dark-colored glass.

What a relief! But what an idiot I'd been—taking up my friends' time, and even getting preliminary estimates for a new water pump. However, I actually enjoyed going back to those I'd consulted, informing them that the "great oil slick mystery" had been solved. Everyone—especially my children—thought it was absolutely hilarious.

I've found that humor opens up my children's hearts. It breaks down communication barriers and creates an atmosphere of openness. A warm smile from "big, strong Daddy" immediately opens a child's spirit. As parents, we need to be full of laughter and surprises, jokes and joy. A heart in relationship with God bursts with gladness and cheer. Humor gives us hope, and hope brings life to the romance.

## "Glad Game" Spirit

We've already looked at the "glad game," the central theme of Pollyanna. This game is really quite simple. When something happens that doesn't line up with our wishes or expectations, we look for anything to be glad about. The more difficult to find the glad thing, the more exciting and challenging the game. Kids play this game naturally but it seems harder for adults.

On one occasion, I had to make a last-minute trip from Denver to Reno. Searching the Internet for a decent plane fare, I settled on a red-eye special with an awkward connection. When my family dropped me at the airport I was sulking and had few words to say as they drove away. A silver lining in the clouds was the furthest thing from my mind.

I had the middle seat in an exit row and figured I would end up claustrophobically squashed—big guys, both sides. It was even worse than I'd imagined. The guys were huge and they both wore black suits. I cringed as they made their way toward me.

To my surprise, after they took their seats, one of them pulled out a Christian book and began to read. I couldn't resist remarking on the book, which he promptly handed to me with a friendly, "Feel free to read it." I soon learned they were Christians returning home from ministering at a conference. One was the basketball legend Meadowlark Lemon; the other was professional football star Earl Edwards.

Sheepishly, I admitted to myself that it was my honor to be in that middle seat. Our conversation continued after we disembarked—in fact, I almost missed my connection.

It was very late when I boarded the next plane. My mood had improved but I still didn't expect another positive segment. However, on this leg I ended up sitting next to a banker who became enthralled with my science. After an entire flight of stimulating conversation, he offered to help me find a motel. He even drove me there. I was speechless.

That two-segment flight, which I'd expected to be an

exhausting ordeal, turned into one of the most memorable trips of my life. God had played the glad game on me. I felt so foolish having shut my eyes to the Larger Story. Then I had to face the embarrassment of explaining it to my family when I got home.

On another occasion, I was preparing for a conference in my hometown. Everything seemed to be going fine—my text was solid and I knew the material well. I'd even written a song to drive the main point deeper into the parents' hearts. Dawson was going to emphasize the message by shooting his bow on stage.

I wanted to do an especially good job, but I came down with a viral throat infection three days before, which left me barely able to speak, much less sing. Dark clouds gathered in my mind, obscuring my vision for what we were trying to do. I was on the verge of depression and anger.

Then I thought: What would Pollyanna do?

It occurred to me that I have a tendency to speak too loud and with too much force. Sometimes I turn people off by coming on with too much passion. The weak voice I was stuck with might be just the ticket, especially in my hometown. It would be painful, but maybe the pain could help me focus. It might even bring a better balance of humility and tenderness to my delivery. I would also have to rely more on God. I began to see something to be glad about.

Dawson was quietly watching my every move.

It turned out to be one of our best presentations ever. Dawson set the scene by nearly doing a "Robin Hood"—hitting the center gold of the target with his first arrow, and nearly splitting it with the second. Then he watched me hang in there as my voice got progressively weaker. There was a strong connected feeling between my material and the audience. I was focused on the message and, as a result, less self-conscious than usual.

I had barely enough voice to finish, and afterward I could only whisper a few words. But since I couldn't talk, I had to listen more. People became more friendly and open, and my compassion grew for them because, instead of half listening while preparing to share my "expert" advice, I heard what was in their hearts.

> "Wow" backwards is still "wow."

When we play the glad game, we look for evidence of the Larger Story in what might otherwise be a difficult situation. I know a large family in which this process is a private joke. The key phrase is, "Oh, wow!"

"Wow" backwards is still "wow," so no matter what life throws our way we can still find the "wow" in it.

## EYE FOR BEAUTY

Last fall Dawson and I were camping at 10,000 feet. One afternoon I realized he hadn't been in camp for several hours so I hiked up the ridge looking for him. I found him sitting on a ledge gazing out on the valley and cliffs, thousands of feet below. At first I wondered what in the world he was looking at. Then I saw the white new snow on the red rock framed by gold aspen quaking in the bright sunny blue of the sky. It took my breath away. No wonder Dawson had sat there for hours.

Sadly, beauty is often hidden in the ordinary routine of life or below the surface. One of my favorite films is *Rigoletto*. Although it was never shown in movie theaters, it's available through the company Feature Films for Families. The main character, Bonnie, is a young girl who's able to see with the eyes of her heart past the superficial ugliness of Ribaldi, a stranger from a faraway place. At one point in the film, Bonnie acknowledges this paradox to her mother: "How could he do something so wonderful if he's supposed to be so bad?" About Ribaldi's beautiful friend (the "princess" in this fairy tale), she asks, "How could someone so beautiful love someone so ugly?"

Her mother answers, "I don't know. Maybe there's something more to Mr. Ribaldi than meets the eye." The story line of this "fairy tale" is filled with poetry and beautiful music that bear witness to the Larger Story:

> *There is no curse or evil spell*
> *That's worse than one we give ourselves;*
> *There is no sorcerer as cruel*
> *As the proud angry fool.*
> *And yet we cry, "Life isn't fair!"*
> *Beneath our cries the truth is there—*
> *The power that will break the spell*
> *We know very well, is locked within ourselves.*[44]

The ability to perceive hidden beauty is a quality of God Himself, who sees even in the vilest sinners and the most horrendous circumstances the potential for good. When we parents exhibit this redemptive quality, children are drawn to God. Hidden beauty revealed is a powerful romancer. It can kindle a desire for God as it nourishes the heart.

But the power of beauty can also make us uncomfortable, to the point of writing it off as earthly or dangerously trivial, for Satan has counterfeited beauty and all but monopolized it for his own purposes. We must reclaim this tool of romance by exposing our children to the beauty of creation, the beauty in the world of human creations inspired by God. We must involve our children in the process of the creating. This process should involve searching for it and bringing it into our homes and lives—on purpose.

We must not cede this God-created glory to the domain of the devil, but instead enter the beauty contest for our child's heart. Fyodor Dostoyevsky said, "Beauty is not only a terrible thing, it is also a mysterious thing. There, God and the Devil strive for mastery, and the battleground is the heart of man."[45]

## TRUSTWORTHY HEART

Once a friend of mine hired a Christian life coach to help her sort out the positive challenges, opportunities, and visions she had for the future. The coach said, "You must put your 'big rocks' in your jar of life before the pebbles, sand, and water are poured in, or the important things will not fit." The coach also gave her a personality test, which revealed a surprising pattern—her mercy and compassion score was essentially zero.

The coach, who was also a licensed counselor, was surprised, although he knew she'd always been awkward at expressing sympathy. He eventually concluded this was a coping mechanism that had probably developed early in her life. Since she was healthy and happy, he didn't recommend therapy.

My friend, after reviewing her childhood memories, concluded this was her way of coping with broken promises. When she was a child, her father talked constantly about all the things they were going to do together. Instead, he watched television. His greatest passion was for the country club culture, so he designed most family vacations around golf. Gradually, the number of promises he broke left all his words hollow and laced with lies.

> My friend's young heart couldn't bear to be disappointed again.

My friend learned never to anticipate or hope for anything, because her young heart couldn't bear to be disappointed again. If she expected nothing, when something did come she would be surprised and happy. She understood and forgave her father, but the memories still left a scar.

Kathy, another friend of mine, once said, "God doesn't tease. He's not like that." She wasn't referring to ordinary play, but to someone powerful playing with someone vulnerable, as a cat plays with a mouse. Trust is incompatible with abusive teasing. Parents often get away with such behavior because children are resilient and responsive, and they forgive easily. But they have their limits, and eventually they do suffer damage— to their emotions, their spirits, their view of the world, and their ability to trust God. A parent's trustworthiness will place either solid ground or quicksand under their child's feet.

Jesus made it clear how serious it is to deceive or lead a child astray. "Whoever causes one of these little ones who believe in Me to sin, it would be better for him if a millstone were hung around his neck, and he were drowned in the depth of the sea" (Matthew 18:6).

## PASSION FOR TRUTH

I love *Meditations on Hunting,* in which the Spanish philosopher
Jose Ortega y Gasset describes his attempts to "hunt down the
hunt." He uses hunting as a metaphor for the search for truth
by describing the hunter as the "alert man" who tries to see all
at once to anticipate where or for how long his quarry will
appear, and exactly what it will look like.

Plato used the hunting metaphor in the same way:

The time has arrived...when like huntsmen, we
[philosophers] should surround the cover, and look
sharp that justice does not steal away, and pass out of
sight and escape us; for beyond a doubt she is somewhere in this country: watch therefore and strive to
catch sight of her, and if you see her first, let me know....
Here is no path...the wood is dark and perplexing; still
we must push on.... Here I saw something: Halloo! I
said, I begin to perceive a track, and I believe that the
quarry will not escape.[46]

Karey and I experience excitement like this in our own
search for God's truth. Karey wrote, "Isn't it in our passionate
pursuit of Him  that we become ourselves? I long...to inspire
and influence my children's hearts with the flame of my own
zeal for life."[47] Proverbs compares the way of wisdom to a
treasure hunt for God's truth and its application to life, the
discovery of which brings great pleasure.

Journaling is a wonderful help in this "hunt" for truth.
Though the word journal usually brings to mind a notebook

filled day by day with thoughts, feelings, poetry, and records, a journal need not be a formal book. Anything will serve—scraps of paper, napkins at a restaurant, brown paper lunch or grocery bags. The only thing that matters is capturing and preserving ideas and insights, which can later be integrated into our personal pursuit of truth.

Our home has nine libraries and many filing cabinets, filled with notes, data, and papers we've gathered over the years. Karey and I love the journey along the way to wisdom—taking anecdotal data, information, and knowledge to a philosophical level, and putting the puzzle together in the context of a Christian worldview. This is the way we've done our journaling. We collect truth, file it, save it, and synthesize it—like Sherlock Holmes and Watson on the trail of a mystery, or archaeologists discussing the results of a dig. It's no small thing when our children witness this. I know our curiosity is contagious, for they all have begun their own search for truth.

Conversations around our dining room table are intense—a "downloading" of our research, our working hypotheses and theories. We love nothing better than to sit for hours discussing theology, science, culture, art—anything involving God's truth and how it applies to life.

We can gather clues from many sources in the search for God's truth—personal experience, nature, sermons—but books are among the richest. This shouldn't surprise us, since God uses a Book as His primary mode of communicating truth. Karey and I drag books all over the house, until we can't walk anywhere without tripping and we have to return some to the shelves. We often wake up with fascinating ideas from our bedtime reading. Sometimes our kids raise their eyebrows at each other, wondering what in the world we're talking about. It's exciting to think of all there is to learn, observe, and contemplate for the rest of our lives.

Karey has always read aloud to our children. We let them have books in their cribs, and often peeked into their bedrooms to see them looking at their books when they woke up from their naps. They learned that books were precious, not to be ripped or marked up. To emphasize this, we never even tore pages from magazines in front of them. They've adopted our attitude in the high regard we place on the written word.

> *It's exciting to think of all there is to learn, observe, and contemplate for the rest of our lives.*

Clarence Cook, in a book on interior decorating in 1878, wrote, "A house without books is no house at all." I readily agree. Don't you feel a warmth in a room with books? I'm drawn to areas filled with books, even in restaurants. Charles Dickens spoke of a little room off his childhood home where his father kept a collection of books. He said they were a constant comfort to him, keeping alive his imagination and his hope in something beyond that particular place and time.

Our family's passion for books, which began when we lived on the road in that crammed Chevy Blazer, has never diminished. We searched out used book sales by calling libraries and women's auxiliary groups, plotting the dates on the calendar. We went with plastic bags and boxes in hand, trying to be near the front of the line when the doors opened. The kids and Karey ran for the children's and youth sections, while I scurried all over. Our plan was to grab all the books that looked old; one person was then designated to guard our stash while the rest kept looking. This person, usually one of the kids, would soon be curled up next to our boxes, deeply engrossed in one of our finds.

All those book-buying excursions, with their rich conversations and shared emotions, knit us together as a family, and gave us so much to talk about. Today, when people tell me they don't know their children, or can't communicate with their teenagers, it wrenches my heart. Travis still calls us from college begging for more books.

Parents can expect to infect their children with godly character and virtue only if they're contagious themselves. What our children "catch" from us will affect their hearts more than what they're taught in more direct ways. Our character is the hammer that drives home the truth of what we say into the minds and hearts of our children. And what we do is a reflection of that character. Methods of romancing our children's hearts are as essential to our role in parenting as tools are to a craftsman.

# Chapter 10

# Methods for Romancers

*Draw them, woo them,*
*And touch them, too;*
*Love them and romance them,*
*'Til we win their hearts for You.*

Saxton Pope—one of the most famous archers in the tradition of Robin Hood—wrote, "A bow, like a violin, is a work of art.... Every good bow is a work of love.... A true archer must be a craftsman."[48]

Using Pope's book as a guide, Dawson and I sculpted a longbow from a seasoned stave of Missouri Osage that had once been a fence post. This golden orange wood is considered the best for making longbows because of its straight grain and resilience. Our challenge was to follow the grain God created in the wood to release the bow that already existed within. Our goal was to "romance" the bow out of the wood. This required vision, patience, and skill, as well as special hand tools: a drawknife, bench vise, spokeshave, jack plane, and a pair of calipers. The tools were essential for us to produce a bow with proper proportions, tiller, symmetry, and arc—one that would brilliantly cast an arrow along the right trajectory.

So it is with romancing a child's heart. The methods of romance are the tools. As in crafting a bow, the key is the skill with which we wield these tools.

## USE ORDINARY OPPORTUNITIES

It's Saturday morning, and I'm engaged in a household project. I discover I need a few more screws from the hardware store. I don't really want to go because it disrupts the project, but if I quietly slip away I could be back in twenty minutes. Like an efficient machine I head for the pickup.

As I back down the driveway I notice my son watching through the living room window, his face squashed against the glass. I can see little round fog rings under his nose. Without doubt, he longs to go with me.

So why not take him? Sitting beside me on the front seat—if I don't turn on the radio—he'll have my undivided attention. He'll know, even if only intuitively, that I value him and enjoy his company.

> Our noble missions steal time that ought to be given to our children.

After we reach the store, we don't go single-mindedly on a hunt for the screws. We do a little exploration. We stop a minute and smell the 3-IN-ONE oil and the new leather of the latest tool pouch. I teach him about hardware and the geography of the store. I ask his opinion. I let him help me find the right screws.

On the way home, we stop at the local ice cream parlor

and sit awhile. I listen to him, look him in the eye, and let the boy in me become friends with my son.

He feels like a prince. Even if he doesn't shout it to the world, he's saying in his heart, "I'm sitting next to my dad and he's my hero!"

So, does it matter that my little errand took an hour instead of twenty minutes? When all is said and done, this small investment will return much bigger dividends than a more "efficient" trip ever could. I might even believe this need for screws was set up by the Author of the Story we're living, as an opportunity for me to romance my son's heart. It happens that way, minute by minute, day by day.

For every little boy or girl in our world, there's a father or mother who can get so focused on achieving life's little goals that he or she fails to see the opportunities to make their child prince or princess for an hour, or a day—and do an eternal work in their hearts. Our noble missions, even legitimate ministry involvements, steal time that ought to be given to our children.

When our daughter Heather was a child, I was helping friends by mentoring a boy named Kevin. I really enjoyed our times together, as he reminded me of myself. One Christmas morning, Kevin's whole family was at our house for breakfast. Karey had made our traditional Swedish potato sausage, aebleskivers, ostakaka, and fruit soup. After breakfast, Kevin, his sister, and I took off cross-country skiing through the woods behind our house. We skied down some old logging roads and headed into the black timber on a steep north slope where the snow was deep. When we circled back to the logging roads, I noticed some little footprints on top of our ski tracks, but I was too preoccupied with my ministry to pay them much attention.

When we got home, Karey asked if we'd seen Heather. My heart sank. I immediately realized the footprints I'd seen were hers, following us. By then the light was fading. I set off like a skier possessed, straight down the hills, through the trees, searching for my lost little girl. I knew she was out there somewhere, up to her waist in snow and at risk of hypothermia as the temperature dropped.

Heather wrote about the experience she had that day in a little book she called *The Mountain Girl Follows Papa:*

Once upon a time there lived a mountain girl named Heather. She followed Papa, Kim, and Kevin. She tried to find Papa, Kim, and Kevin, but she didn't at first. She had her boots on and followed their ski tracks. She heard Papa's, Kim's, and Kevin's voices down in the spring and went through the barbed wire fence. She went to a cliff and found ribbon on a stick. She went to the end of Papa's tracks and stopped...[She] went up to the tree and started to cry.

She went to the tracks again and followed the tracks all the way to another barbed wire fence. The snow made her shiver and cold and she was tired of walking and was too tired to step any further. The snow was past her knees.

By a very large woods she stopped and listened and heard wild dogs. She broke a stick off with her hands because she wanted to hit the dogs with it. She was so scared. Then she heard Papa's voice and she whistled for Papa and Papa got her on his back and he walked up the hill with her on his back. Then Papa skied down the mountain with her on his back....

Travis and Mommy said they had prayed for Heather and she was glad they did because what if wolves came or she was scratched by a panther, then Papa never would have his Heather back.

I'd overlooked the opportunity to share an experience with Heather on Christmas morning, of all times, to try to minister to two other young people. However noble that other task might have been, it left my young daughter with an overwhelming longing that drove her to search me out and left her both physically and emotionally vulnerable. You can imagine how I would have felt—how I would still feel today—if Heather's guardian angel hadn't led me to her that day, just before dark.

A minister friend of mine wasn't so fortunate. One day, he and his three-year-old son, Jonathan, were riding in their car, talking about this or that, when they passed a dead deer by the side of the road. All at once, their conversation took a different direction. "Daddy," Jonathan asked, "if I was killed, would you still be able to find me?"

It was a golden opportunity to talk about eternity and faith, and a whole range of related things, but my friend figured there would be another time for that, and he changed the subject. He didn't know that in less than three months Jonathan would no longer be with him, and he would be left forever wishing he'd followed his son's questions wherever they led.

If we're wise we'll make the most of every opportunity, knowing the days are evil (Ephesians 5:15–16). The evil one will steal away opportunities if we let him. Even interruptions can be opportunities. If they irritate us and we ignore them, we may be missing the best blessings in life, because they may have more to do with God's plans than with ours. We need room in our lives for relationships, or we miss the best part. Richard Swenson says, "When God taps us on the shoulder and asks us to do something, He doesn't expect to get a busy signal."[49]

The same should be true for our children when they tap us on the shoulder.

## TELL STORIES

In the May 26, 1982, issue of the Chicago *Journal,* an article described children's answers to the question: "What would happen if there were no stories in the world?" One child said, "People would die of seriousness." Another said, "When you went to bed at night it would be boring, because your head would be blank."

Storytelling is an art form we all practice, a craft that's accessible to virtually everyone. The narrative world is dynamic, fluid, and by definition relational. Stories are nets that catch truth, and they're mirrors that show us truths about ourselves. Stories are both hygienic (healthy) and therapeutic (healing). Jay O'Callahan, a storyteller from Massachusetts, said, "Storytelling is a kind of music with the storyteller as the instrument."[50] And the melody romances the heart.

Norma Livo and Sandra Rietz describe "storying" as "a vehicle for transcending time, for binding people together with the future, the past, and one another, for extending commonality of experience, for ordering events to make existence more sensible and meaningful." In storytelling we bring "a higher level of comprehensibility to the things we do" because "we join with others emotionally and intellectually, and we generate a sense of 'rightness' and belonging."[51]

Storytellers are found everywhere. In Elko, Nevada, are cowboy poets. On the front porches of Tennessee are grandfathers. In Lake Wobegon is Garrison Keillor. In pulpits across America are preachers. In the diners of North Dakota are farmers. In Hollywood is George Lucas. At the Rendezvous in Fairplay, Colorado, are mountain men. Storytellers have always been there.

In the early twentieth century, children performed recitations and monologues in schools and libraries. Storytellers traditionally were trained at home as the art passed from generation to generation. "Oral" households were characterized by a family storytelling tradition featuring a story hour, usually at night around the woodstove. These times knit families together, created lifelong bonds, and romanced children's hearts to God's truth. But storytelling has suffered a serious decline since the advent of television. Our hearts and our hearths have grown cold.

> Most people,
> especially parents,
> are natural storytellers.

Most people, especially parents, are natural storytellers. Around a dinner table, fireplace, or campfire, stories roll off our lips—about our families, our friendships, our lives. So we should have no difficulty telling stories to our children. This makes us vulnerable and produces an intimate "from my heart to yours" feeling. It goes far in teaching character, in bonding and developing intimacy with our child. Writing a story down saves it and is important, but telling it brings it to life.

This does not, of course, mean we should pour out our whole past to our children—mistakes and all. We don't want our children to desire, or feel they have the right, to follow in our wayward footsteps. Some parents seem to enjoy bragging about their youthful sins or, worse, use their children as therapists as they unload the garbage of their past. Discretion and common sense are in order.

I believe it's the father's responsibility to establish a storytelling tradition for his family. This may involve controlling, or even getting rid of, the television. I like the way this is expressed in the song "Once Upon a Time":

*Daddy was a family man and the only way he knew*
*To entertain the children when Ol' Man Winter blew*
*Was to sit them down and gather them around that great big fireplace,*
*And say these words as he watched the firelight flicker on each face.*[52]

If our grandparents are still alive, they also have lifetimes of stories to tell. Their stories can provide children with a sense of history, conveying truth, adventure, beauty, and drama, romancing their hearts to God. Grandparents who have lived without God also have valuable stories to tell. Often these point clearly to God, offering us a golden opportunity to share with our children in private about the way God leads or provides, even when the people involved may not recognize His care themselves. The relational linkage children can develop to their family roots through such stories provides them with a sense of security when the storms of life rage, and a sense of home no matter where they are. It gives them a more complete perspective and a more accurate picture of the Sacred Romance—a God's-eye view of life.

In the past, such interchanges between generations took place around the family dinner table. Today, complex family schedules have made the dining room table a nostalgic memory in many homes. This may be one of the most damaging blows the nuclear family has ever experienced. It's another reason for shutting off the television when we're together, so the natural flow of conversation around the table will be stimulated toward, and flavored with, storytelling.

All we need to do is ask the right questions, direct the conversation, keep it uplifting and edifying, and make sure no one's left out. When a story begins, encourage the child to tell it in detail.

In *Endangered Minds,* Jane Healy wrote that an executive mind (in the good sense) is created through dialogue between a parent and child. The disappearance of the dining room table correlates with the appearance of what she terms "McLanguage." Verbal fast food, she says, consists mainly of inflection and gesture: "Its like...(shrug). You know, like...." Healy adds, "Because the development of human language is the foundation for the development of human thought, this sloppy syntax is a symptom of a serious problem—kids don't think."[53]

When adults engage in passionate philosophical conversation, children are all ears, and when we ask them their opinions, the answers are often profound. They have a knack for speaking truth directly and clearly when adults might hedge. By including them in our conversations, we build important relational bonds. It lets them know we respect their opinions. This is especially true in the presence of guests. The phrase "children should be seen and not heard" is so wrong. It depreciates children to something less than persons of worth. We need to welcome children into the conversation. In their childlike hearts they'll think they're adults (people) among adults (people) doing adult (people) things. Before we know it they actually will be adults, and we'll harvest what we've sown.

When we have guests for dinner, there are obvious questions to ask, which will stimulate all kinds of stories: "How did you two meet?" "How did you get into that career?" "What's it like to live in Brazil?" "How did you come to know the Lord?" In this way, we also teach our children, indirectly, good conversational etiquette, by focusing the discussion around our guests rather than ourselves.

> *One way to begin is to tell our children our own life story, right from the beginning.*

Our own children, as they grew, lingered longer and longer around the table. They would leave and then come back, and eventually they would stay. Many times we've been spellbound, or we laughed so hard we literally cried, as we listened to our guests' stories. Even dreams can be realized around the table. It can be a place of romance in more than one sense. Scott and Christine Dante express this truth well in the words of a song:

*So we never got to Paris*
*And found the café of our dreams*
*But our table holds a whole world of memories.*[54]

Fathers, let's make storytelling a priority in our schedules. One way to begin is to tell our children our own life story, right from the beginning, a chapter a night. Our parents can help by filling in details we don't remember.

It takes creative and emotional energy to tell a good story. If we're running on empty in other areas of life, we need to pull back and simplify, so we have something to offer from the recesses of our hearts.

## ESTABLISH FAMILY TRADITIONS

Our greatest challenge in romancing our child's heart is to continually live in the Larger Story. The spiritual discipline of celebration, expressed in family traditions, is designed to help us do just that. Celebrations remind us of God in our midst. They give perspective and lift our eyes to the Larger Story.

The word holiday is derived from "holy day"—a special day set apart for a spiritual purpose. The primary purpose of these times was to point to the Larger Story through celebration and feasting, usually around the family table. Praise of God was the focus, arising not out of duty or obligation but out of joy. Relationships developed as God's love, care, and will were communicated in a clear, dramatic style.

Celebrations like these write memories on our children's hearts. Children are visual, physical, emotional creatures. Specially dramatized and visualized "holy days" are highly effective in affirming their faith, as we communicate what we believe through reenacting historical events.

The first five books of the Bible are called the Torah,

which means "guidance," "direction," "instruction," and "information." The word teach in these books means to repeat God's truth by telling it to our children as we sit in the home, walk by the way, lie down, and rise up. Devout Jews wrote His words on the doorposts of their homes. Our aim as parents is to etch the truth on the doorposts of our children's hearts.

When our children see, hear, smell, taste, and feel the Word of God, it becomes part of them. As they participate through our traditions, they enter the Story. This isn't some make-believe play—it's reality for a Christian, because it connects us to eternity past and brings God's mighty works throughout creation and history into our lives. We should be saturating the atmosphere of our homes with God's presence.

The word remember occurs over three hundred times in the Bible, indicating the importance of sharing and reminding our children of God's truth through the telling of His Story. Zakar is the Hebrew root word for "remember" and "memorial." Another meaning from this root is "one who remembers" or "remembering one," implying we're the ones who carry on the story.

God instructed the Hebrews to use traditions, remembrances, and reminders to teach their children. As an old proverb says, "Put something where you can see it, so your eye will remind your heart." Traditions build feelings of security in a child, and our relationships with our children grow as we experience things together. Traditions say we all belong to something bigger—something of deeper significance than Santa Claus or the Easter bunny. Our shared experiences will draw them in, captivating their affections and romancing them to God.

Even a good tradition can become routine, especially if parents shoehorn themselves and their children into it out of a sense of duty. Legalism and empty ritual are often the result. For this very reason, the Lord says, "I hate, I despise your feast days, and I do not savor your sacred assemblies" (Amos 5:21). We tend to fall into routines, forget about His Story, and get carried away with the busyness of life. Our traditions soon focus on propositional truth, doctrine, and theology. If this happens, they become dry, oriented to formula instead of relationship, and lose their real meaning.

One way for families to combat this danger is to create their own traditions. I inherited several that Karey and I have observed with our own family. When I was a boy, my parents celebrated Christmas in the tradition of their Swedish Christian parents and grandparents. Christmas Eve was a special and sacred family time, focused on Jesus. For days beforehand they prepared special foods to set the day apart. The preparation heightened everyone's anticipation of the celebration. And they made the most of what they had.

There was a shortage of meat in those days, so they mixed it with potatoes and made a special potato sausage. They took bones and the little meat remaining and simmered it all day on the wood-burning cookstove. During the mealtime, the family lined up and dipped bread in the broth. This dipping party, called duppa i gryta, communicated unconditional love and family unity. They had special rice pudding and fruit soup for dessert. Papa read the Christmas story from the family Bible, and the presents were opened that night.

My parents adapted these traditions, and Karey and I have expanded them. For example, the first present we open is the family Bible. Our latest addition is our "third day of Christmas" smorgasbord—a whole day dedicated to ethnic foods and fellowship. We spend the day reflecting on our human heritage and contemplating how God has worked through it. We invite friends of different backgrounds to share their histories. We exchange stories about God's hand in our lives. Times like these around our dining room table are times of authentic fellowship, offering a glimpse of heaven.

Another tradition we created for our family is celebrating our children's spiritual birthdays—the anniversary date when each received Christ as personal Savior. The featured activity is a treasure hunt for our meal, which is either Colorado-style tacos or curry. These dishes have many condiments, which can be hidden throughout the house, with clues. The children go from clue to clue, searching until all the food has been found. Children love the challenge of solving the puzzle by reading the clues, trying to find the pieces that fit. When the pieces are all found and put together, we have a complete meal, during which we recall past treasure hunts and remind them of their treasure in heaven. The conversation is directed to sharing their testimonies.

Tom Strong and his family live north of Cheyenne, Wyoming, along the Platte River, a locale famous for its blizzards and arctic air. When Tom noticed how their Christmases had become too focused on the gift process, he moved the opening of gifts to a week after Christmas so the family could focus on the birth of Christ on Christmas Eve.

Tom also proposed that the family make a stable, and sleep in it on Christmas Eve. To his surprise, they agreed. They borrowed thirty or forty hay bales from their horses, and built an eight-foot-square shelter with a makeshift roof in their front yard. The family began Christmas Eve by walking to neighbors' homes and singing Christmas carols. Later, they piled into the cramped "stable" for the night. At one in the morning, Mom went back to the house; their daughter and her friend from college followed at two-thirty, joining Mom for some hot chocolate. But Tom and the three boys spent the whole night in the stable.

They woke to fresh snow. Tom wanted to do some teaching, but by then he realized they'd already learned far more through their senses. The vivid experience brought home to them all the real meaning of Christmas.

## Share Unique Experiences

Sharing unique experiences romances the hearts of everyone involved. We're connected to our friends and family by facts or beliefs, but also by experiences we've shared. They're links in the chain that forms the story of our lives. The more unique, unusual, and vivid the shared experiences, the stronger the links. The most traumatic, challenging, exhausting, exhilarating, scary, mysterious, and costly experiences are the ones we remember best.

Why not design these unique experiences with your children? Shock them tonight by pitching a blanket tent in the living room. Then crawl in (you won't even have to ask your children to join you) and read them a book by candlelight. The next step is actually to go camping. Camping is one of the greatest ways to bond as a family—just you against the elements.

One time, our family went camping with Karey's cousin Terry, his wife, Joanne, and their children. We did a pack trip with horses up one of the northern canyons of Colorado's Red Table Mountain, to a secluded aspen grove. Terry and I had bowhunted there for elk, and we wanted to share the area's beauty with our families.

We loaded two horses and started up the mountain—children, moms, dads, and a shaggy white dog named Partner. We had about a half mile to go to the campsite when it began to rain hard just as we were crossing a steep, bare clay slope. The horse I was leading started to lose its footing. The saddle and panniers, with about two hundred pounds of gear, began to slip off its back. I stepped below the horse to try to adjust the saddle, which slipped down over the horse's tail and back legs to the slimy ground. (Outfitters use chest harnesses on pack-horses to prevent this problem, but we hadn't thought of it.) At the same time, Terry's horse, a young spirited mare, began to buck and slide down the slope, dragging Terry along behind her. Fortunately, since the horse I was leading had only one eye on the uphill side, it couldn't see the disaster unfolding and did not panic.

I was in a dangerous position, holding the saddle with one hand so it wouldn't roll down the mountainside and pushing on the horse with the other so it wouldn't roll over me. One slip and a thousand pounds of horse would have planted me in the mud. As I looked up at the kids slipping and sliding, dressed in makeshift rain gear—black plastic garbage bags—and Karey and Joanne trying to stand in place, I thought all was lost. But somehow, Terry calmed down the mare and came to the rescue. I have no idea how we ever got that saddle back on my horse—

or rather, how Terry got it on, because it was all I could do to push on the horse to keep it from sliding down the hill.

After reaching a less slippery spot, we turned around to see the most incredible rainbow arching across the narrow canyon below us. Above it the sky was a dark bluish black, and below it the sky exploded with dazzling golden brightness. We were all speechless with wonder. It was a scene and experience we'll never forget.

On another occasion, Dawson and I spent a cold June night on a lake in Utah. At midnight we were bowfishing for carp with a close friend, a champion carp shooter. Dawson was only about nine, so this was a huge adventure for him.

This wasn't the best night for it. The water was murky and almost freezing, and eventually I gave up and huddled out of the wind. But Dawson never quit. He stood the whole time on the shooting platform in the biting wind, armed and ready with his little bow. In reality he had about zero chance of hitting a carp—the bow was too weak, the distance too far, the carp too small.

*Someday we'll look back in wonder at how God included us in the drama of history called His Story.*

Why was he so serious in these terrible conditions? Because my friend and I had invited him into our adult world and Dawson was making the most of it. Our getting skunked was irrelevant to Dawson, because for those hours he was one of us. I'm sure he never wanted it to end.

Such experiences become primary links in a powerful chain of eternal moments—each lived in the present—that form the permanent memory collection we call life. They link us to those who will come after us, starting with our children, and to those who have gone before. And someday, I believe, we'll all look back in wonder at the way God included us, by His grace, as players in the drama of history called His Story.

## ALLOW FREEDOM AT HOME

My mother met the challenge of keeping house for four very athletic sons with her usual artistic panache. We were programmed to be physical, she reasoned, and to fight or try to control this innate tendency would frustrate us and distract us from our schoolwork. So Mom and Dad boy-proofed the house to relieve our stress and save Mom's valuable antiques. They bought two sturdy four-legged end tables and two metal lamps. They threaded the lamp cords through holes drilled in the tabletops, and bolted down the lamps. Of course, when we knocked over a lamp the whole table fell over, but it was easy to set it up again. The most humorous part of the whole thing was that the first "boy" to overturn this ingenious device was Dad. When it happened, we all looked at Mom to see her reaction—a smirk, then a smile, then laughter. She was indeed a kindred spirit with all her boys.

The floors were similarly durable: hardwood, linoleum, tile, and the toughest industrial-grade carpet obtainable.

Our boy-proofed house still had unmovable boundaries our parents set for us. Grandmother's antique curved-glass china cabinet symbolized one of those boundaries. It was left in the house, filled with delicate dishes, vases, and bowls, many of them from Sweden. By God's grace that cabinet was never touched, even when my youngest brother convinced Mom it was essential for him to practice dribbling his basketball indoors. To help his team win the high school conference championship he simply had to hone his ballhandling skills through continuous practice on the hardwood floor.

Perhaps Mom was a bit weary after raising three boys already. Or perhaps she was still experimenting with parenting strategies. At any rate, she said, "As long as you don't bounce the ball off the walls." Believe it or not, no basketball or baseball ever touched that china, which still survives in my parents' house despite frequent visits from three generations of kids.

The bottom line in such matters depends upon our highest objective as parents. A mother once told me, as she reflected on raising several sons, "If I had it to do over again, I wouldn't spend as much time cleaning the stove. I would spend that time with my boys. The stove is long gone and nobody really cares anymore how clean it was."

Some of Karey's favorite sayings are: "Dust is country"; "Cobwebs can wait, but children's hearts cannot"; and "It's not clutter, it's creative activity." Her priority is family, relationship, and creativity. When we built the house we now live in, we designed it around food, music, and books. We built an informal bed-and-breakfast suite for guests. Hospitality is our priority. We've pushed this philosophy to the limits, but every time we do we end up with a little taste of heaven.

For four years, we hosted a family camp. Each time, sixty people stayed for a week. I had to build a bunkhouse for the girls. The boys slept anywhere they found themselves when they were ready, while the parents pitched tents and set up trailers. We rented portapotties. Karey still has dreams (nightmares?) about preparing food for that mob. We thought hosting so many people for such a long time might put our house at risk, but it recovered. Most important, family, friendship, and fellowship flourished.

It's important to our children how their parents relate to their friends. Travis and Heather will often bring them home—sometimes ten at a time—to sample Mom and Dad's cooking and the home atmosphere. We always try to engage their friends in philosophical conversations while asking them to tell us their stories. When their friends are gone, Travis or Heather will always ask us, "Well, what did you think of Josh (or Shelly)?" Our response usually leads to a deep conversation.

Recently, Dawson asked me if he could hang his sparring bag—an old canvas duffel bag he'd stuffed with basketballs, volleyballs, and soccer balls—in the house somewhere so he could practice his tae kwon do. He said, quoting me, that the only way to exercise consistently is if the equipment or the place is convenient. At first I hesitated; then I realized it could hang from a beam in our great room, away from the furniture. It worked fine, and he's able to practice his moves every time he walks by the bag. It has also turned into a hit with visitors. It isn't a permanent fixture of course, but I suspect that someday, when Dawson is grown up and has left home, we wouldn't mind seeing it swinging there, with another little boy kicking and punching it.

My sister-in-law Chris, who has adopted a similar approach to atmosphere and freedom in the home, wrote this story:

It was a typical morning. I woke up, rolled out of bed, walked to the bathroom, looked in the mirror...and "they" were there. I quickly put my contacts in and went outside for some fresh air on the deck. As I opened the patio door I gasped as I saw "them" again.

I hurried back to the kitchen for a drink of water. I peered out the window at the fresh new day and again "their" presence greeted me. I bolted for the front door to see if I could escape, but as I was leaving "their" numbers seemed to multiply.

Outside now, I opened the van door and quietly slid inside. Closing my eyes I sat paralyzed, half in fear and half in hopeful relief. I lifted my head and, as the early morning sun shone through the window, I could see "their" shadows falling across my body. In a gesture of bold surrender I looked around, and yes, "they" were there—before me, beside me, and behind me, on each and every window.

I hung my head as I realized that, for this mother of four boys, there is no escape from fingerprints.

What a picture of a home! Her boys inhabit every square inch and she loves it.

Once I was talking by phone to my cousin Bekki, who lives on a dairy farm in northern Wisconsin. I asked her something about parenting and family lifestyle, and she began laughing. "What's so funny?" I demanded.

Bekki said, "Oh, it's not your question—it's the answer." And she painted a picture of her eighteen-month-old son, Moses, sitting on the linoleum floor pouring a gallon of maple syrup over his head, then happily splashing, slapping, and trying to swim in it. Rather than getting upset, Bekki savored the sweet moment.

I'm not recommending parents provide their children with jugs of maple syrup with which to experience sweet moments. However, Bekki's answer illustrates what comes to mind when I think of a home atmosphere that contributes positively to romancing a child's heart. Children need a safe, secure home in which they're free to relax and be themselves—free to create, laugh, and cry. They need a warm-hearted, reasonably well-functioning, cheerful home, where they can let down their guard, take off their masks, and be nourished, fed, and rested. My uncle once said, while visiting the suburban foothills of Colorado, "These people build houses for other reasons than living in them." I think he meant that some people lead sterile, deprived lives in houses filled with material luxury—all the while longing for real homes.

> *Children need a safe home in which they're free to create, laugh, and cry.*

## BECOME A KINDRED SPIRIT

When Dawson was ten, I took him with me to have our bikes tuned up for his birthday party—a mountain bike trip in and around Moab, Utah. Several fathers and sons were going to join us, camping in the high desert and riding some of the best trails in the world. I'm not much of a mountain biker, but I recognized Dawson's love for the sport and his need for supervision.

Visiting the bike shop was a great experience for Dawson, but the main point was that his dad was excited about the same thing he was, and we were doing it together.

Dawson had visited the shop with Travis when he was only

four. I asked him to direct me there, making him more than just a passenger as we drove. He couldn't remember the exact location but helped me look for the sign. When we rolled our bikes in, I told the owners, "We're here to have you tune up our bikes and to get some instruction in shifting. I want to bike the backcountry with my son. The last time I rode a bike was ten years ago and I never got it out of high gear. I pedaled up a mile-long hill and was sore for a month." They laughed, and we talked bikes for half an hour—Dawson, the bike shop owners, and me.

Then I noticed they rented telemark skis and boots, so I asked, "If you had a ten-year-old son, would you start him out in telemark or downhill skiing?"

Telemark was the unanimous choice. We then had a great time dreaming and planning with Dawson concerning the best way for him to develop skills in this lifelong sport. The focus was on how Dawson and I could ski together. After discussing pros and cons, we decided we would stick with cross-country skiing for a couple more years before taking up telemark skiing.

I asked about avalanches and Dawson heard stories of drama and danger—the stuff dreams (or nightmares) are made of. The men told Dawson he needed to begin studying avalanches now if he planned on someday skiing steep chutes with deep powder in the backcountry.

As we drove home, Dawson was at peace with the world. The process of dreaming, preparation, anticipating adventure, and tangible action with his dad had brought genuine contentment to his boyish heart. You could see it in his countenance.

This is the goal in relationship—journeying together, not

simply arriving at the destination. I had shown up, and he had owned the adventure with me. I'd shown him respect. He knew the object of my affection was more than mountain biking or skiing or even him. It was our friendship, our camaraderie, our partnership. We were kindred spirits because our objective was sharing passion, hard work, and creativity. This fundamental principle is so easy to overlook, even when we have the best of intentions. It costs more—of our time, energy, and money—but is definitely worth it in the end.

As parents, we must part with our adult agendas and embrace our child's dreams and plans if we desire to be kindred spirits. When children share music, a book, or an idea, they're looking for our approval, support, and respect. We need to see things from their perspective, to walk in their shoes and empathize with them.

My brother Scott has sons who excel in the all-American sports of basketball, football, and baseball, all of which he loves. However, when one son took a liking to soccer, which Scott never played, and for which he had little affinity, he said without hesitation, "If my son likes soccer, then I like soccer."

Scott is a creative father. He loves to fish, something that never attracted his older boys. But they all love snorkeling, so Scott combined the two—they fish underwater. Although it's hard to cast, they've had incredible success. Recently I was riding in his minivan and asked him what the odd smell was. "Oh, it's just a frog," he said. "It escaped out of my pocket and we never could find it." I'll let you decide if the frog was bait or a catch.

When Travis was still too young to drive, he was the worship leader for a local youth gathering. Every Monday night I drove him up a road with many switchbacks to the barn where they met on top of a mountain. Instead of simply waiting or returning home, I took Dawson with me. This became our night out. Dawson always ran in with Travis for a few minutes to socialize with the high school kids (especially the girls—they loved him). But his main motivation was to pick up a fresh doughnut. When I finally got him back in the vehicle we drove down to Baskin-Robbins, where we sat and licked a couple of cones and hung out together until it was time to pick up Travis.

Kathy, a close friend of ours, is mother to eleven children. It takes ingenuity and insight to connect personally with each child, and she shared with me that sometimes the most obvious way is to look into their eyes. Eyes truly are the windows to the soul—they reveal the heart, and a child will know by our eyes that we can be trusted. Kathy and her youngest son have a morning "gazing time" when she looks deeply into his eyes with a lingering look of fondness, humor, and enjoyment. She has done this with all of her children since they were babies. She tries to catch each of her children's eyes when they approach to let them know uniquely they're the one she loves and wants to know.

We need to take advantage of every opportunity to relate one-on-one with each of our children. It's hard to romance a child's heart in a group.

## BE WILLING TO SACRIFICE

As I entered my teen years, I became increasingly involved in activities outside our home. New, attractive voices were enticing me away from my family and the values I'd been taught and absorbed through my upbringing. My parents, who for so many years had nurtured my passion for God and His creation, saw the danger. They knew they could shelter me for only so long. So they became aggressive out-romancing the other suitors of my soul.

They developed a literal "where the rubber meets the road" strategy. One thing they did was let me pick out our new family car when I was in junior high. I'll never forget that ivory-colored 1963 Dodge slant-six. My criteria for choosing it were sleek looks, sleek looks, sleek looks—so even though it was the best car we ever owned, I got no credit for that. I used it in college, as did one of my brothers, and we drove it well over a hundred thousand miles.

Allowing me this much freedom came so naturally to Mom and Dad that today they hardly recall it. But I do. And it means as much to me today as it did then. They wooed my heart by listening to me, believing in me, trusting me, then following through by putting their money—literal, hard-earned cash—where their respect was.

> They let me pick out our new family car when I was in junior high.

I still use the dictionary my parents bought me for college in 1966. Both covers are gone and it's barely holding together, but whenever I look at it, I think: They worked hard for the money they used to buy me that dictionary. It's a symbol of the sacrifices they made to ensure that my brothers and I got college educations.

My brother Mike married into a family that has lived for generations on a beautiful island in Lake Michigan. The island is thirty-six miles around, a fact he knows because he once ran the perimeter in a single day. Mike and his wife, Linda, know everyone on the island, where friendships and relations run deep and strong, and there's a strong sense of community. They gather for music Friday nights in an old red barn, and sometimes have "Door County fish boils"—a famous community tradition.

Mike's expertise with computer software means he has many business opportunities that would require a move to another part of the country. He's also a gifted Bible teacher and speaker, and has had attractive offers in full-time ministry. But he's chosen to stay close to his family. In fact, Linda and Mike chose the town they live in based on its location— halfway between the homes of her parents and ours. Their children have greatly benefited from the deep roots they enjoy with family and friends. In Mike's case, this sacrifice has had a significant role in winning his children's hearts for God.

Another brother, Skip, has bowhunted elk for several years. The hunting hasn't been successful in the normal definition of the word. But Skip has succeeded in a much more important way, because he has exchanged the likelihood of bagging an elk for the pleasure of taking along his oldest son on almost every hunt.

Bringing anyone along in this sport greatly decreases your chances—but it increases your collection of stories, as each participant experiences each challenge uniquely. Together, Skip and his son have called in giant bulls, but always something happened to spoil the shot. Once, a bull was tearing up a tree with his antlers, bugling right in Skip's face, but he was on the wrong side of the tree trunk for a shot. Another time, Skip shot and a pinecone happened to fall from the tree at that particular instant, deflecting the arrow—or so he claims.

Together, father and son have camped in rain, snow, and fog, miles from nowhere. Once they had to "swim" out through four or five feet of snow. But my brother has told me, "I don't care if my freezer isn't full. I won my son's heart."

Skip and his wife, Cindy, have applied this same principle in relation to sharing life with all their children. My niece wrote down some of her recollections:

The Suburban was silent as the snow fell outside. My dad looked at my mom. What is there to say when you slide across a bridge and over a cattle guard on the ice? Even less when the cow on the other side totals the vehicle! We were stranded five miles from home on a back road in Wyoming, in the middle of December.

"Well," Mom said, "we still need to get there."

"There" in this case was one of a hundred events the eight of us kids participated in. Someone still had some-place to be and, in my family, short of someone bleeding, we would manage to make it. The plan evolved. Dad was wearing dress shoes, as was Mom; my brother, who was wearing sneakers, was the same size as Mom. He elected to go stocking-foot for a time (rather than slip into her heels), giving Mom his shoes so she could jog the ice-covered gravel road in the dark back home to get our other vehicle. We were late, but we got "there."

When we first started homeschooling, Mom vowed that her children, while not having phys ed built into their school curriculum, would not be physical "morons"—a concept that won our hearts as we began trying and excelling in every sport (every sport quite literally meaning every sport that exists). I don't know how many times she must have regretted uttering those words. With at least half of us in different sports at any given time, she got creative. Coaching soccer teams means you can set the practice schedule, which in turn means you just might be able to coordinate with baseball. Coordinating with baseball means you have only two trips to make into town daily, rather then three, and only one meal a day to eat in town rather than two. Of course, all is null and void when the all-star season begins.

Ten thousand bratwursts and burgers later, we know every park in town that has BBQ grills where we can eat "family meals" between practices. Add an equal number of miles to the Suburban, resurrected after the near-fatal brush with the cow, and the hours my mother spent playing "super-soccer-baseball-softball-swimming-football-basketball-(you get the picture)-mom," and they begin to add up to astronomical proportions. We never felt unsupported. And my twenty-one-year-old brother still calls home to ask, "Mom, are you coming to my game?"

## ENCOURAGE A GOOD PATH

My friend Jeff was running errands. He had his three little girls with him. Even as they began, the girls were already tired and wanted to go home. On the first stop, Jeff had his youngest daughter in one arm and a bag in the other. His oldest daughter said, "Uppy, Uppy!" which meant she wanted to be held. Since Jeff couldn't hold her, she had a meltdown.

Back in the car, heading for the next stop, the girls were either whining or crying. Instead of fighting them, he said, "Wouldn't it be funny if we did all the rest of our errands backward? Who's with me?" They ended up playing a wonderful little game together that produced some comical looks on the faces of people they met along the way.

> *Distracting a child from bad paths is a powerful parenting method.*

To encourage a good path, even distracting a child from bad paths, as Jeff did, is a powerful parenting method. Research has shown that the most successful parents do this. When children stray off the good path these parents gently woo and direct their children back. The more time children spend on the good path, the more they'll feel at home there and the less they'll be drawn to the way of fools.

This is the same principle used in training bank tellers to recognize counterfeit bills. If they're truly familiar with the genuine article, they'll naturally recognize the counterfeits.

## HELP THE HELPLESS

Once Travis traveled to Mexico and helped build a house for a family. In an essay describing this experience, he wrote:

Sitting on the motel bed eating pizza, I started thinking about little Julio, and I felt ashamed. My primary thought since the storm had been washing a little dirty water off my leg. Julio's house was so flimsy. If that storm had blown my tent down, what had it done to his house? Was he still out there wrapped in plastic and shivering in the rain? Did the flood carry him away? I suddenly lost my appetite for the pizza in my hand. I quietly put it back in the delivery box and walked out into the rain.

I began to understand now why I had taken this trip. I thought about how many other Julios there were out in the storm, and all over the world. I realized that this problem is too big for me. I became angry and then frustrated. Soon I sank into a helpless despair. All the things that I have filled my life with seem trivial compared to the needs of Julio. As the rain stopped, my emotions calmed. Then, like the night sky that had cleared, my mind cleared itself of the confusing thoughts that had filled it. I realized that I cannot change the world by myself, but while I was in Mexico, I helped change the world for one child and his family.

Mission trips to third world countries often move the heart in ways no other experience can. I've seen hardened young hearts profoundly touched and turned toward God. In extending kindness to those who cannot repay it, something moves the heart. Helping hurting people during the 9/11 tragedy stirred the soul of America.

James 1:27 says, "Pure and undefiled religion before God and the Father is this: to visit orphans and widows in their trouble."

"Orphans and widows" can be considered a metaphor for the helpless. In Luke 14:13–14, Jesus says, "When you give a feast, invite the poor, the maimed, the lame, the blind. And you will be blessed, because they cannot repay you."

Chapter 11

# The Sense of Wonder

*If I've lost my sense of wonder,*
*What's the sense in living at all?*
*When the child in me can't remember,*
*Or hear my little boy's call?*

"Fires of His Wonder"

At a conference that was drawing to a close, I wandered over to a window. The verdant green of a soccer field stretched out before me in the summer sun. Then I noticed a mud puddle near the sidelines. A little boy sat in the middle of it, wiggling his barely visible toes in the chocolate water. Applying some secret logic that only little boys can understand, he'd put his shoes and socks at the edge of the pool, completely clean and dry, while the rest of his clothes were being soaked as he splashed and laughed his way to paradise.

A knowing smile crept across my face as I watched. After a while, I realized that a woman standing beside me was watching the boy, too. I assumed she was his mother, but no hint of disapproval or reprimand clouded her face.

I turned and asked, "Who taught you how to romance your son's heart like this?"

She remained quiet for several moments, gazing out of the window. During this time, my question lingered in the air and seemed to wither. Then she responded as if I'd asked the most natural question in the world. "Ever since his little brother died from leukemia last year, I see things differently."

Her voice trailed off. A shadow of painful memories crossed her face. "I've learned the difference between things that matter and those that are incidental. He's with me and we love each other—that matters. A little dirt and water don't. He's just a little boy loving God's creation in a way that makes God smile—in a state of innocent wonder. Who am I to rob them both of this pleasure?"

As she walked away, she said with a whimsical shrug of her shoulders, "After all, you can always wash a pair of jeans."

A temporal perspective would see dirt, germs, and inconvenience. This wise woman's viewpoint tells the Larger Story—that eternity intersects time when a little boy wonders that his toes can wiggle even when he can't see his legs. From an eternal perspective, we see a child's fascination, curiosity, amazement, and breathless enchantment at a creation with God's fingerprints and brush strokes all over it. With all that at stake, why would we rush to extricate our children from muddy puddles or syrup spills?

Children smell, touch, feel, hear, and see nature as if it were creation's first morning. Eternity and the sense of wonder are connected, because nature originated in the eternal creative heart of God. This single fact alone should arouse our sense of wonder as well as our children's, as they instinctively sense that the world isn't ordinary but a work of art. They're drawn to it as to a huge, captivating drama, for creation constantly shows us the divine fingerprint. It's a book written by God, showing us glimpses of the Larger Story and eternal mystery.

Of all creatures, only humans are capable of wonder, of feeling excited by something unknown or miraculous that's beyond our comprehension, our control—beyond the comfort and safety of our rational adultish world. To "halt in amazement" is how the Dutch philosopher Cornelis Verhoeven described wonder. He suggested that the event of wonder is inserted into the middle of movement and brings a momentary pause to thought. When we halt in wonder, we instinctively "hold our breath"—which then "catches in our throat." This pause, for a Christian, is in actuality a form of worship.

> *Children experience nature as if it were creation's first morning.*

According to Plato, wonder is the beginning and cause of philosophy. Wondering at the changing nature of things led Plato to assume the existence of the eternal, imperishable, and transcendent. This perspective implies that philosophy is something that's "done" rather than simply "known." Socrates said, "The sense of wonder is the work of the philosopher. Philosophy indeed has no other origin."

Verhoeven, in *The Philosophy of Wonder,* gives larger meaning to the word than is traditionally embraced. Wonder, he writes, is not "a quasi-romantic, wide-eyed passivity" but "an aggressive action, an exciting adventure, an exercise in free fall." His definitions include many biblical elements: Wonder is "the principle, the basic structure...not only the beginning, but also the end." Wonder "guides and accompanies thought.... It has not only the first but also the last word."[55]

Wonder is only a heartbeat away from worship. It's the natural reaction to belief in God and the awareness that He's the Creator of time, space, and matter. Wonder is a prerequisite to worship. Scripture tells us that almighty God is worthy of worship because He's the Creator of all things. We honor Him when we live gladly in a state of wonder because of His works, the most wondrous of which is that humans can have an eternal relationship with Him.

Children wonder naturally, but adults soon teach them to end this esoteric pursuit. Most children's sense of wonder is crushed or lost by the time they reach third grade, through a secular culture that brings futile and cynical despondency into their once wonder-filled lives. When they become adults they tend to fall into routines, grow complacent, and lead pragmatic lives. They grow up, and as they get bigger, everything else gets smaller. Words like *blasé, worldly wise,* and *sophisticated* describe grown-ups who have become adultish, and have stopped asking "silly" childlike questions.

Mike Starkey says that "the effects of the sixties' libertarian revolution [loss of wonder] were a little like bludgeoning Santa Claus to death in order to get at the presents immediately."[56] This is the natural consequence of a generation living out the secular worldview of our culture. Without God, there's no Big Story. Without story, wonder is quixotically absurd, leading nowhere. Our culture has lost its sense of wonder because it has lost God.

The closer we are to God's absolute truth, goodness, and beauty, the more we wonder, regardless of our age. Charles Dickens, writing of children, said it's no slight thing when those who are "fresh from God" love us. But the Age of Enlightenment narrowed our vision through its fragmented microscopic view of the world. According to Peter Kreeft, it was as though they "screwed down the manhole covers on us so we became squinting underground creatures."[57]

Einstein felt that anyone who could no longer feel a sense of wonder was as good as dead. Often, when I make a discovery in my field of science, I'm left stunned with wonder. All I can say is, "God is here!" I sometimes feel like a child playing on the beach, as described by Sir Isaac Newton, looking for pretty pebbles while there's a whole ocean of undiscovered truth lying in front of me.

> *Because children live in the present, they savor the moment and the sheer sensory experience.*

Children are spontaneously and naturally drawn to things that make them wonder, especially God's creation. Because children naturally live in the present, they savor the moment and the sheer sensory experience. Perhaps this is why Christ spoke of the ideal of childlikeness. When children wonder at the world around them, they may be the closest of all people to comprehending the reality of God. Often this is expressed by a wide-open mouth. They believe in Story—in the sky, in the rocks, in the water, in the trees, and in the animals. This captivates them, draws them, and romances their hearts.

Childlike wonder is also characterized by trust in the order of things, because God is almighty and has a good heart. These foundational assumptions undergird childlike faith, for without them wonder degenerates into helpless bewilderment. Astronomer Jean Picard said wonder is fatal if it isn't assimilated. Wonder must be connected to the Larger Story or it will lead nowhere, leaving the wonderer to despair.

Wonder is the essential instrument of the poet, artist, scientist, and any other creative thinker. It incites the mind to organize information and ideas into pattern and form. Perhaps adults cease to wonder out of fear. They don't wholly trust that God will provide a happy ending. They were taught to trust, instead, in rational logic. This "sophistication" short-circuits their wonder, and they're afraid to be carried away into the unknown. They would rather hold their own flashlights, instead of holding God's hand and following Him through the darkness.

Wonder runs through Scripture, leading us to one reality— the worship of God. "Stand still and consider the wondrous works of God" (Job 37:14). "Lift up your eyes on high, and see who has created these things" (Isaiah 40:26). "When I consider Your heavens, the work of Your fingers, the moon and the stars, which You have ordained," David, the shepherd-king says to God, "what is man that You are mindful of him, and the son of man that You visit him?" (Psalm 8:3–4).

David's son Solomon was a naturalist. "God gave Solomon wisdom and very great insight, and a breadth of understanding as measureless as the sand on the seashore. He described plant life, from the cedar of Lebanon to the hyssop that grows out of walls. He also taught about animals and birds, reptiles and fish. Men of all nations came to listen to Solomon's wisdom, sent by all the kings of the world, who had heard of his wisdom" (1 Kings 4:29, 33–34, NIV).

Clearly, God's creation is far more than just a pretty backdrop to life. Getting to know the creation firsthand, and searching for truth as we walk the way of wisdom, should be one of the most natural pursuits of believers.

For many of us, the most vivid memories we have from childhood involve nature. Ask little children what they like most and it will usually be things like dirt, flowers, rocks, horses, water, volcanoes, dragonflies, and dinosaurs. Most of us as children had a natural attraction to the earth—an insatiable desire to explore and to have adventures. This force drove us and filled each day with newness and wonder. Nature's stories wooed and romanced us to God, even if we hadn't been taught about Him and it was only an indefinable longing. Our natural awareness grew, fueled by the fascination we had for God's handiwork.

A lot may have changed since we were young, but children haven't. Our children probably also have an insatiable desire to experience and to explore nature. We can help them with a "sense of wonder" curriculum.

## EXPERIENCING NATURE

Hands-on experiences allow our children's sense of wonder to thrive and grow. Children who touch rocks, catch butterflies, and watch clouds become naturalists in the whimsical sense, whether they choose science as a vocation, hobby, or simply as a vehicle to deeper worship of God the Creator.

We can feed our children's sense of wonder through a systematic, hands-on exploration of the earth. How simple or varied this will be depends on where we live, our ability to dovetail their exploration into family vacations, our willingness to travel, the age of our children, and, to a lesser degree, our finances. But we can all begin in our own backyard or the local park. What's essential is that parents and children experience nature together.

A "curriculum" to cultivate a child's sense of wonder should be centered around all five senses. Children need to see, smell, hear, touch, and taste God's creation. In this phase, our goal is experience, not analysis.

I recommend a curriculum organized around the spheres of the earth: the atmosphere (air), the hydrosphere (water), the lithosphere (crust), the athenosphere (mantle), and the biosphere (life). This will give a broad and balanced coverage of creation, while sparking ideas for other areas of study.

To experience the atmosphere, consider a hot air balloon or airplane ride, watching a sunrise or clouds, flying paper airplanes or a kite, photographing lightning, or chasing a thunderstorm. Experience the hydrosphere through canoeing, fishing, watching waves, wading, swimming, and walking in the rain. Discover the lithosphere by spelunking (cave exploration), mountain climbing, rock collecting, and backpacking. Dig a hole, build a snowman, visit a quarry, or ride a bike. To learn about the athenosphere, visit a volcano, visit the Yellowstone geysers or lava flows, or soak in a hot spring. The biosphere is probably the most readily approachable wherever we live: keep a pet, go hunting or bird watching, climb a tree, pick raspberries, garden, cook a meal.

> *Let their sense of wonder resuscitate your own, and you'll have a great time.*

Such activities bring parents and children together into direct contact with nature. Unless children ask for facts about what they're experiencing, these aren't the times for scientific lectures. Our primary role is to participate in a childlike way, by engaging our own five senses and our hearts in a shared, uncomplicated experience.

This isn't always as easy as it sounds. Last winter, Dawson and I were driving past Evergreen Lake when we saw some ice fishermen. Dawson begged me to stop, and we walked down to the edge of the lake. I felt conspicuous without any fishing equipment, so I sat on a bench while Dawson stepped onto the slushy ice. To my surprise he didn't walk up to the fishermen. He just wandered around, poking sticks down abandoned fishing holes, sliding, and examining the textures in the ice.

Finally, when he'd talked me into joining him, I understood what was going on. The fishermen were secondary to his fascination and wonder focused on the lake. He then asked if we could try ice fishing sometime, and I said I had great plans to take him to a lake about an hour's drive away, where I knew there were huge northern pike. He said with a sigh, "Papa, let's just fish here."

I'd missed the point. He didn't need a special lake with giant fish; he just needed a lake. All I had to do was let his agenda become mine, and let his sense of wonder resuscitate mine, and we would have a great time—as we always do when I allow this to happen.

As we cultivate our child's sense of wonder, our own sense of wonder will be stimulated, too. We'll become like children, enjoying again those things that the responsibilities of adulthood have crowded out of our lives.

Thomas Carlyle said the tragedy in life isn't what we suffer, but what we miss. We need to learn how to see, how to sense, how to be aware of what's going on around us—the small, simple, ordinary, everyday things. If we're doing that, we'll be able to answer questions like these:

What cloud types were in the sky the last time I was outside?
What weather did they indicate might be approaching?
What smells were carried by the wind?
Which way was the wind blowing?
What flowers were in bloom?
What birds were singing?

If the answers are all a mystery, we need to get reacquainted with our senses. We can enter our child's world only if we're tuned in to our surroundings. Dawson prefers to sleep outside for most of the summer, and he would in the winter, too, if we'd let him. He wants to be immersed in nature—luxuriating in the fresh, mosquito-free, Colorado night air. Modern culture and society have lured many of us away from nature and from using our senses. Television, computers, the four-walled comfort of our houses, our luxurious cars—all have dulled our senses. Distinctions that were sharp to us as children are now but a blurred background for our stark, pollen-free, scentless adultish reality.

The most fascinating aspect of Y2K (besides its being the most significant nonevent of the twentieth century) was its function as a wake-up call to people who had come to rely nearly completely on society and technology for their needs. Many had forgotten that a loaf of bread begins in a wheat field; that clean drinking water is not a luxury but an everyday necessity; that apples on the supermarket shelf come from a tree, and the milk from a well-fed cow. Forgetting these realities has weakened our connection to the earth. We're divorced and disconnected from true creation, as we live in a world we think we created.

Most of us have a vast knowledge of our popular culture,

which we consume in earnest, but we're embarrassingly ignorant of the world God created. While nearly everyone can name those famous cereal characters—Snap, Crackle, and Pop—few can walk down the street where they live and name the flora and fauna that make their stroll so enjoyable. John Muir inspired his daughters to learn the names of the trees in their garden by saying, "Don't you like to be called by your first name?"

Participation with a child in the activity of wonder will romance that child's heart—if we avoid sermonizing. "Billy, see the pretty bird God made just for us to see" forces a dutiful response to our dutifully given theological explanation. On the other hand, a spontaneous expression of genuine wonder and curiosity excites a child's interest and points inevitably to God in a way that woos rather than repels a young mind. "Wow! Look at that hummingbird!"—as it dive-bombs your heads—"I wonder how it can fly like that—up, down, sideways, any which way it wants. I wonder if it can fly upside down?"

These comments may lead you to read descriptions in guidebooks or to visit websites on the Internet (such as www.hummingbirds.net), where you can learn any number of things about the seventeen species in North America, or the three hundred and twenty species worldwide, of the bird family Trochilidae. For now, however, the "Wow!" will suffice.

> *Dirt is good for children.*

While we're encouraging our children to touch the creation, they're bound to want to sit in a mud puddle from time to time. If we really want to impress them, we'll jump in with them. It's worth doing just to see the look on their faces and feel the camaraderie. Mud, dust, sap, sand, bugs, soot, and plain dirt don't hurt anyone. In fact, a recent *Science News* issue promoted the idea that dirt is good for children—which every kid knew all along.

The article "Germs of Endearment" reported that by raising barricades against deadly scourges such as smallpox, typhoid fever, and polio, we've shielded people from microbes and parasites that don't harm us. Scientists now suspect (keep in mind that this is preliminary, and the problem is extremely complex) that stamping out innocuous organisms and separating people from dirt in antiseptic environments is weakening some parts of children's immune systems while other parts grow unchecked. This, they theorize, causes an imbalance, triggering asthma, allergies, and even autoimmune diseases such as rheumatoid arthritis and the most severe type of diabetes.

Studies have found that hay fever is less common in children raised on farms than in urban areas. Also, children in large families, particularly younger siblings, have fewer allergies than children from smaller families. This suggests that germs travel downhill; those brought home by older siblings may protect younger children by strengthening their immune systems. Antibiotics—especially when administered before age two—may be killing off beneficial bacteria, spurring some immune disorders.[58] So a little dirt is important to the health of children.

Had we known this, we might not have hindered two-year-old Travis's attempt to strengthen his immune system. We were living west of Tucson in the desert mountains. It was spring and I was tilling some manure into our garden. I'd brought Travis down from the house and set him under a

Paloverde tree in an open area away from the manure pile. The sandy, gravelly ground was dry, and he seemed content to watch a covey of quail walking around with their new chicks.

I was preoccupied but suddenly noticed how quiet Travis had become. When I glanced over, I saw that his mouth was full of something. I ran over and, to my shock, realized his little hands and mouth were packed full of rabbit droppings. They were well-seasoned and dehydrated, and I hadn't noticed them when I set him there. I'd kept him away from my manure pile, but he'd found his own.

Poor Travis—the next few minutes must have been bewildering for him as I scooped him up and ran to the house, all the time pulling rabbit droppings out of his mouth. Then he had to endure having his mouth washed with soap—not once, but three times.

There's an irrepressible attraction between little children and dirt. Dawson enjoys dirt even more than I did as a child. Once, we flew to Florida from Denver via Dallas. In the Denver airport, when Dawson stood up to board the plane, though he'd taken a bath the night before and was wearing clean clothes, the seat he left behind was covered with sand. Then in Dallas he sat down waiting for our connecting flight, and when he stood up there was more sand—a lot! By the time we got to Florida the sand was appearing in smaller quantities. To this day we don't know where it all came from. It would have been more understandable if we'd been traveling the other way, from Florida to Denver.

Tools of all sorts—nature guidebooks, rock hammers, hand lenses, butterfly nets—all help our children explore the spheres of the earth. If they learn, through our participation and guidance, to become good observers, skilled in collecting specimens and data, they'll rise naturally to the more technical level of pattern recognition. When they want to go beyond merely experiencing the earth, it's time for unit study.

## EXPLORING NATURE

Unit study can come in a variety of shapes and sizes. The best are delight-driven, because these flow from our child's natural inclinations and curiosities. When children's passions are ignited by some interest, then the study is personalized. They own it, and end up investing much more energy in the study than they otherwise might. Unit studies can be called special projects, hobbies, research, or play. In one case, we called ours "The Flowers of Evergreen."

When my mother was a young girl in Wisconsin she was enthralled by the song "Springtime in the Rockies" and the vision it brought of mountains, meadows, and flowers. Little did she know that someday her eldest son would raise his children in Colorado. I love to call my mother when springtime comes to the Rocky Mountain meadow that is our front yard, and tell her the first flowers of the year have bloomed. Her girlhood dream has come true through her son.

One spring, our family decided that instead of just looking at the flowers in our meadow we would study them, photograph them, smell them—get to know them firsthand. This experience was like examining the brush strokes of a master Artist, who over the next few months painted our meadow with delicate, extravagantly beautiful flowers—some of which bloomed for just a few days until, to paraphrase Psalm 103:15–16, the Chinook winds blew and they were gone and their place remembered them no more.

But we remembered them—more than two hundred in all. Our study began when Travis (eight at the time) informed us that a purple pasqueflower had pushed its way up through the melting snow. I grabbed my camera, several flower guidebooks, and a notebook. Karey, Heather, and I then followed Travis through scattered snowdrifts to the first flower of the year.

Artistic photos of wildflowers generally emphasize color. But form and texture are also important because they're the keys to identification. These are captured best in black-and-white photos, or in sketches. This is why many flower experts take great pride in their ability to draw flowers.

Travis carefully sketched the pasqueflower as Heather recorded information in our notebook: date, location, and flower name. With camera in hand, I ended up lying down and crawling around on my elbows on the wet, gravelly ground until I'd framed several pasqueflowers in my viewfinder. We soon learned that, to examine and photograph a flower properly you must contort your body into myriad uncomfortable positions for agonizing periods, to get the flower positioned just right for its portrait.

By the end of the spring we had an amber haze of pollen hovering over our meadow. But not until green clouds of pine pollen began to drift by did anyone feel any hay fever symptoms. The pollen can become intense when you spend day after day eye to eye with flowers.

We noticed immediately that bees were often interested in the same flowers we were photographing. It's a good idea to consult your doctor before embarking on a study like this, to ask if you should have a dose of epinephrine on hand for possible allergic reactions to bee stings. These are rare, but they can be deadly. Somehow we escaped bee stings, even though we had ten beehives of our own at the edge of the meadow.

In these intimate studies of nature we must always be prepared for the unexpected. One afternoon, we discovered endangered Colorado orange red wood lilies blooming around our spring. As I knelt down to photograph a flower, I was interrupted by a loud squeaking sound, which came from a very large mouse being swallowed by a very small snake. One of the strangest and funniest sights we ever came across was a stump sporting a crew cut—hundreds of golden hairlike strands sticking out of its top, which turned out to be a squirrel's hoard of grass seeds, stored in an amazingly orderly way for the winter.

Age level and natural science aptitude determine how sophisticated your study will be. Since our children were under ten when we did the flower study, we limited information collection to identification and the time of the first flower's appearance. Had they been older we would have included such things as temperature, rainfall,

> *In studying nature, always be prepared for the unexpected.*

length of blooming time, and flower color. The more information, the more patterns we see and the more science we end up doing. Science is simply the pursuit of knowledge through observation and experience, pattern recognition, and the organization of this information into a story.

During a study like this we'll be led down occasional rabbit trails. For us, one of them was the gathering and preparation of wild greens for a salad, which is a custom in France. We recommend doing this one in moderation—we found that our family's digestive systems weren't accustomed to so many vitamins and nutrients in such a concentrated form.

This experience didn't discourage us. Tasting edible flowers and plants became one of the highlights of our study, and gave us great respect for Native Americans and early settlers, who relied on wild plants as an important part of their diet. It also gave us a sense of self-reliance, since understanding what is edible in the wild is a practical survival skill.

Travis learned that one bowl of kinnikinnick berry soup for breakfast curbed his hunger for the whole day. Although it tastes like green apples, this concoction isn't half bad if you pretend to be starving. Although most wild plants are edible, a few are poisonous; therefore, the ability to identify them is all-important. When in doubt, don't eat. If young children are involved in the study, clear and careful instruction is advised.

Another highlight for us was collecting and drying the flowers. About the middle of the summer, when our meadow had become a kaleidoscope of colors, Karey began carefully picking flowers to dry. We discovered two traditional drying methods. The first requires a drying agent such as silica gel or smooth beach sand (mortar sand is too abrasive). We used silica gel from a craft store. Flowers are placed in a box and the sand (which must be dry) is gently poured around and over the flowers. In a few days the sand will dehydrate the flowers. Once the sand is gently removed we're left with a perfectly dry preserved flower. In most cases the color is also preserved. We made some beautiful arrangements of dried flowers.

Flowers can also be dried in a flower press, which is two nine-by-twelve-inch pieces of wood with wing nut screws at each corner. Place the flower between the boards along with some cardboard to absorb moisture, and tighten the screws. After a few days the dried flowers can be mounted behind glass in a picture frame for wall hanging, or mounted on heavy paper as a page in a notebook of flowers.

Karey also gathered flowers and other plants, particularly seedpods, and hung them in bunches to dry. These were beautiful works of art in themselves, and added a nice aroma. She used the dried flowers to make wildflower wreaths, which she hung on our porch and throughout our home.

Our family persisted in documenting flowers through late spring snows, monsoon thunderstorms, hot and dry summer days, and finally, September frosts. We rarely missed a day. Although our goal was to complete the study, our greatest joy came during the process of search and discovery.

After the last flower—a showy aster—had caught the frost and withered in late September, we began organizing our slides and information, grouping the more than two hundred flowers we'd identified by the month in which each first appeared. It was fascinating to research the origin of a flower's common name and the folklore attached to it. This gave us a wealth of material for a colorful slide presentation. Karey and I helped with organization, while Heather and Travis wrote the text. They eventually presented the show to their grandparents, friends, and local community groups. Encouraged by the positive responses, we contemplated publishing a flower guide for Evergreen, but the cost of doing it in color was prohibitive.

The key to fun, successful unit study is to recognize that

each child has unique interests. We can't and shouldn't try to write the script for them. God already has.

A few years after Heather and Travis completed our first flower study, I suggested to Dawson that we do one with him. "No, thanks," he said. "I've already started my own."

"But you don't understand," I argued. "We'll learn all about edible plants, and we can collect specimens."

"Papa, I know all about the study Heather and Travis did. But I want to do one on bugs."

Today the main attraction for guests in the Swan home is Dawson's insect collection. It's a work of art. All the insects are

> *Each child has unique interests. We shouldn't try to write the script for them; God already has.*

professionally mounted and labeled. He uses a black light and a white sheet to attract moths at night. He sets his alarm clock to wake himself up at certain times to check the sheet. One summer our family drove from Denver to the West Coast, then back across the continent to the East Coast before returning home to Denver. Every night, we went to sleep with swarms of insects landing on the black light–illuminated sheet.

Dawson collected and collected. One night, I drew and colored a huge moth on cardboard, then cut it out and pinned it to the sheet while he was asleep. He got the surprise of his life when he checked his sheet the next morning. I loved the grin he had for me when I asked him if he'd caught anything during the night.

Recently, Dawson scheduled us to spend three nights in southern Arizona with his entomologist mentor and colleagues. They use powerful mercury-vapor lamps to attract insects at night. Dawson had to obtain a permit for this world-class collection area, so he could pursue his treasures.

I could fill a book with the experiences from that expedition. Insect nightlife is spectacular and mysterious. The first night Dawson and a gargantuan long-horned beetle collided. Dawson was knocked down and the beetle knocked out. The same night hundreds of huge silk moths came to Dawson's sheet—Eacles imperialis oslari, Citheronia splendens sinaloensis, and Automeris pamina—some of them sporting seven-inch wingspans. We were both enchanted as they silently came to the light, and spellbound as bats periodically snatched them out of the air. The next day we joined a professor and his students hiking and collecting reptiles and amphibians in a remote Arizona canyon. Incidentally, I never pictured myself carrying a butterfly net until this trip. Now I never leave home without one.

> *Anybody can design a treasure hunt for kids.*

## TREASURE HUNTING

Our pastor, Peter Hiett, who has a degree in geology, wrote in a letter to me: "In Proverbs 25:2 we find these words: 'It is the glory of God to conceal a matter, but the glory of kings is to search out a matter.' Does that mean creation is like a treasure hunt arranged by a loving father? I think that's what the fathers of the scientific revolution thought.... Science at first was worship. I think worship is wonder, and wonder is the obvious response to glory."

I'm sure God experiences joy when we explore and search His creation, because I know the joy I've experienced in creating treasure hunts for my kids, then watching them follow the clues.

One day when Travis was about ten, he came up to the house with an ancient ax. The handle was weathered to a thin skeleton. "I was building a fort next to the ledge when I found this! You said Jesse James used to hang out around here. Do you think this might have been his ax, Papa? Do you?"

We were living on an old Colorado ranch in an area that had been one of Jesse James's old haunts. At that moment, an idea crystallized in my mind—to design a treasure hunt and keep this excitement of discovery and imagination alive as long as possible, while at the same time teaching Travis and Heather a little history, orienteering, biology, logic, reading, and research.

I shook my head slowly, pondering the possibilities. "I don't know, Travis," I replied. "But it sure looks like it's old enough to have been here when he was alive."

I spent the next three days secretly placing leather map fragments, antique bottles, artifacts, and a sealed wooden box containing nineteenth-century coins wrapped in an old canvas bag, in various places near the spot where the axe had been found. I chipped clues into cliff faces and glued moss back on to give the clues the appearance of age. When I was finished there was a hand-sculpted bear track at the spring hole and a bottle carefully placed under the roots of a tree, among the clues and along the trail to the treasure.

As the day of the hunt approached, the sense of anticipation I experienced was intense. I suggested that Travis and Heather invite two friends over and the stage was set. When the children arrived we had lunch together, then I nonchalantly said to Travis, "Why don't you see if you can find some more relics under that rock ledge where you found the ax? Here's a shovel you can use."

In a moment, the four children were transformed into explorers, archaeologists, and adventurers. I followed at a distance, not wanting to miss a thing. When they discovered the first old bottle with the map fragment in it, and an Indian Head penny, they entered another world. They truly believed for several days that they'd found the treasure of Jesse James. They had a wonder-filled day, and mine was just plain wonder-full.

They had such a great time that we began writing a little book together, complete with maps and illustrations, telling the treasure hunt story. Then the little book started to grow, as if it had its own life. All that's missing now for this story to become a historical novel for children is some research on nearby gold-mining towns. Now, doesn't that romance your heart a little and tap into your sense of wonder?

Anybody can design a treasure hunt for kids. Start by discovering some local lore with a little mystery (or invent some through storytelling), then develop a hunt that will test the participants without frustrating them. Success depends on the combination of just enough suspense and difficulty to keep them wondering, plus an increasing set of rewards to keep them motivated to reach the final goal—the treasure.

The last time we did a treasure hunt, since Dawson had caught on, I surprised him with a comical twist. The "treasure" at the end of the hunt was a case of Rawhide root beer (a locally brewed beverage) that I'd buried carefully, remembering to replace the sod over the hole. "Papa!" Dawson exclaimed when he discovered it, and I said, "Let's go up to the house and make root beer floats."

Two to four children is about the right number to keep them working together to find a prize that none of them might find alone. If they can learn this valuable lesson about creative cooperation early, who knows what they'll be able to discover or achieve as their sense of wonder encounters God's treasures over a whole lifetime.

As parents, we have the responsibility and privilege to protect and cultivate our children's sense of wonder. Fortunately, God has made this easy through the beauty and intricacy of His creation. Our role is to provide the opportunity for them to experience and explore it—and to share these endeavors with them as fellow treasure hunters (sometimes called "scientists"). God will do the rest—for us, and in us.

> With a quiver of arrows, a dog at his side,
> The sun on his shoulders, a gleam in his eye,
> The whimsical wisdom he shares with me,
> Paints a picture of life, it's somethin' to see.
> He builds forts in the trees and forts underground,
> And some out of old aspen logs.
> His goal's in the making, the building, creating,
> And not in what's finished and done.
> And when the fires of his wonder warm my soul,
> His honest brown eyes let me know.
> I'll hold this moment as long as I can,
> For it may never come 'round again.[59]

# Chapter 12

# The Creative Image

*Holy, holy wind,*
*Let Your passion rise again;*
*Lover of their souls,*
*Set a fire in them.*

"COMPOSER OF THEIR SOULS"

There's a place, an enchanted place, down near our spring, cradled by a granite ledge. Here, an aspen grove meets a stand of giant blue spruce and Douglas fir. In this small, secluded meadow edged with a raspberry patch and carpeted with purple violets, we found the name for our home—Singing Springs. Often I've dreamed of building a log cabin there, with a porch for sitting and songwriting, for creating and contemplating. I put it off partly because I have so many projects on the go, but partly too because I didn't want to disturb the pristine beauty God placed there. But every time I walk down the path that takes me to the forest beyond, I design and construct this cabin in my imagination.

So when I heard about the newest fort Dawson was building "down by the spring," I went to investigate.

The most delicately beautiful part of "my" little meadow was a big mess. Scrap lumber, even particleboard, had been dragged in from some construction site and was strewn about, crushing the tender spring grass and wildflowers. The beginning of a frame was taking shape. The design was "pole barn, circa 1970." It wasn't square or level. Sixteen-penny nails, painstakingly driven, held it together.

At first, shock and disgust froze my heart with anger. But soon the ice melted as the reality of my little boy's passion swept over me like a sweet storm. He'd begun construction with the best materials he could find, following his own original design. He'd placed it not just anywhere in my meadow but in the best spot—the spot that even the designs in my imagination refused to consider because of its "sacredness."

> If we're created in His image, then we must be creative.

As the fires of his wonder warmed my soul, tears welled in my eyes, and it dawned on me: This is the creative image of God incarnate in my little boy! He had made this pristine place a holy place. I joined in God's joy, and smiled and smiled and smiled.

Dr. Paul Brand and Philip Yancey, in their book *In His Image,* tell us the image or likeness of God in which we were made is not our physical shell of bones, muscle, and skin. Our body is simply a vessel, a repository, for God's image, which is nonmaterial. Although there's no consensus among theologians, the image of God in us is probably a combination of attributes, including our ability to reason, spiritual facility, capacity to make moral judgments, and the capacity for relationship.[60]

Dorothy Sayers has stated, "When we turn back to see what He says about the original upon which the 'image' of God was modeled, we find only the single assertion, 'God created.' The characteristic common to God and man is apparently that; the desire and ability to make things."[61]

God's creativity is the central theme of the first chapter of the Bible. God created time, space, and matter out of nothing—ex nihilo. Then He created us "in His own image" (Genesis 1:27). Both Old and New Testaments emphasize that we're God's "workmanship" (Ephesians 2:10). The Greek word *poeas* is the root of our English word poetry. Thus, in a sense, we're God's poetry, which is just another way of saying the image of God in us conforms in part to God's attribute of creativity—the desire, ability, and need to create. If we're created in His image, then we must be creative.

The creative image of God in us is difficult to define absolutely, because at best it's but a poor reflection of an infinite reality—an attribute of God. What we do know is this: To be creative is to have the ability to bring into existence, to cause, or to make. This power is expressed in designing, inventing, shaping, and organizing through imaginative skill and ingenuity. This ability is innate in humans, transmitted to us from God. The creative image is a representation, likeness, or copy of the original—a similitude of God's creativity.

In a very real sense, discovering and developing this attribute is central to finding success and fulfillment in life, because most interesting, important and "human" things result from creativity. Burning curiosity, wonder at mystery, and delight at finding a solution that makes order visible— all these accompany creativity. Our fullest happiness, greatest passions, and deepest satisfactions on earth come during the creative act.

Creativity causes the spirit to sing because it brings relief from the fear that no one is out there. The discovery of order—cosmos out of chaos—floods us with peace, hope, and joy. Order is evidence for God's existence. This reality slices through the veil of despair and boredom that shrouds our fallen nature, giving us a lightning-flash glimpse of true reality—the Larger Story. Creativity is a powerful tool for us to wield in the competition for our children's hearts. Cultivating the creative image of God in them will draw them to the true Source of what delights them most.

Creativity reveals itself most visibly in the fine arts, performing arts, literature, and crafts, but is present even in the "hidden art" of everyday life. Although not traditionally acknowledged, it's also present in science, engineering, athletics, business, and politics.

The creative image of God in us demands expression. When we create we comprehend God better—even feel a holy camaraderie with Him. We own the process. This is a powerful reality. Children long for this ownership when they say the revealing words, "Let *me* do it."

As I see it, the process of creating is as much the goal as the product of the creative effort. The journey is actually the destination. The story told by the process gives our creativity value, purpose, and ultimate meaning. The mere fact that we can create at all is evidence of a divine blueprint, not only for each of us personally but for all humanity.

## CREATIVITY AND CHRISTIANITY:
## DISAVOWING THE DIVORCE

The creative aspect of the image of God in man was laid aside and largely ignored by Christians during the twentieth century. What attention it did receive usually revealed an awkward and estranged relationship. The roots of this tension can be traced to the Enlightenment, when art and religion began to separate. Eventually, a split developed—the art/religion marriage that had once produced great works ended in divorce. In response to the separation, Christian culture elevated functionality to its highest aspiration, and creativity in every sphere was neglected.

With Christianity no longer the driving force and inspiration behind music, art, literature, science, and social reform, Christianity began to be truly marginalized in our culture. Today, our efforts are centered primarily in the humanitarian and moralistic arenas. We've invested our resources and focused our creative imagination on mass evangelism, and have become watchdogs of the moral conscience of the culture. These are legitimate endeavors, but where is the witness to God's creative nature and His passion for beauty in a world that was made to be dazzled by these aspects of Him?

The first persons recorded in Scripture as being filled with the Holy Spirit were the artisans and craftsmen God ordained to fashion the holy vessels and furniture for the tabernacle. Aaron's priestly garments were to be designed for "beauty and holiness." Beauty thus bears witness to the character of God, and art is an ordained way to bear this witness. Art lifts us beyond the physical world, building a bridge to the spiritual realm. Since all our thoughts of God by definition are analogical, the creative imagination provides a blueprint for building this bridge.

But where beauty is viewed as nonessential by many Christians—a worldly extravagance that believers don't have time to indulge in as they work for God's kingdom—the secular world, particularly in the arts, science, entertainment, and the media, is largely devoid of Christian influence. To the degree we boycott involvement in these areas, the competition wins by default. We forfeit our children's creative desires to the adversary because we offer no appealing alternative.

Our children's hearts are naturally drawn to the challenge and fascination of creating and to the beauty the world deceptively presents. How can we romance our children if we aren't in the contest? God is the Creator, Artist, and Author. All we need to do is show up. We have the advantage in this arena, but if we abdicate the romance of our children's hearts in the name of pragmatism and a misguided sense of morality, in the end we'll essentially hand the prize to the competition.

## PROTECTING THEIR CREATIVE IMAGE

Often Christian parents don't recognize the need to protect the creative image of God in their children, who are then left unprotected as cultural noise bombards them from all sides, assaulting and corrupting their imaginations. The noise desensitizes and robs them of their innocence, then misdirects their creativity. I've already mentioned how it seeps into our homes through television, videos, video games, popular music, and music videos. Many of these electronic entertainments leave children mesmerized and, curiously, bored yet hyperactive. They bypass consciousness, inducing a trancelike, passive state—the opposite of the state of mind required for God-honoring creative activity.

Earlier, I addressed—in the context of sheltering and protecting our children's hearts—the physical, emotional and moral battering children suffer from the media and from their peers. The same principles apply to protecting the creative image of God in them. We need to be diligent guardians of their creativity, so that beauty, drama, happiness, and adventure remain in their lives as they grow, and can someday emerge to be a witness to the world.

If our children's creativity points them to God, revealing Him as its source, it will play an important role in the romance of their hearts. But if they grow up entertained by profit-hungry third parties, our children will become creatively constipated, their minds and hearts stagnant receptacles instead of fountains of creative energy bringing joy to themselves and to those around them.

I don't enjoy reading or writing about these dangers, or dwelling on them. There are many books on this subject, and for good reason—our children are under assault. I particularly recommend: *Saving Childhood* by the Medveds, *The Hurried Child* by David Elkind, *Endangered Minds* and *Failure to Connect* by Jane Healy, *Children Without Childhood* by Marie Winn, and *The Disappearance of Childhood* by Neil Postman.

Ironically, the most dangerous threat to the creativity of children may come from their own parents, who have the power to build up or tear down. Children who are ridiculed, put down, or ignored may eventually stop creating, or may never begin. As their emotional tank drains to a dangerous level, the creative impulse in them may eventually shut down.

In contrast, affirmation strengthens a child's creative image. Our children need to know we approve of and value their creations. Setting them up with the tools to pursue their interests sends a message that we believe in them and are willing to invest in their creativity, giving them a sense of security and the freedom to be themselves. Encouragement protects—in a sense immunizes—them against the negative messages they'll inevitably receive from the culture around us.

> *The most dangerous threat to the creativity of children may come from their own parents.*

## MAINTAINING A CREATIVE ATMOSPHERE IN THE HOME

Perhaps the greatest gift we can give our children to protect and nurture the creative image of God in them is the freedom to be themselves—unafraid to create, uninhibited to imagine, to feel, and then to find God's calling for their lives.

The atmosphere in a home originates in the hearts of the parents. When children are secure in knowing we won't ridicule or reject them, but will accept them for who they are, the creative image in them flourishes. When we treasure their creativity and their creations, we bring them not only joy, but also the confidence and freedom to discover the expression of God's creative image in them.

Creating this kind of environment takes time, energy, and willingness to invest our resources. It also requires commitment to the process of romancing our child's heart to the Source of all creative endeavors.

One project Karey and I worked on with our children was binding their stories into books. When they were young, they dictated their stories to us and we wrote them down. Taking that time, valuing their words and their stories, sent a clear message to their hearts. One particularly unusual book that Heather, who was seven at the time, wrote and bound is entitled *The Pond's Puns.* It's a great example of what can happen when we turn off the television, limit other amusements, and encourage a child to let her creativity flow:

Once upon a time there was a pond: a clear, cool pond fed by several springs. He had lots of friends, mainly kids, who would just sit around talking to him, eating their picnic lunch, and figuring out what to do. Lots of kids liked to swim in him in the summer or ice-skate on him in the winter. He was so popular that kids from all over, from different states, and even different countries, came to visit him to keep him company and to learn what ponds do.

One day in the spring the pond was visited by some men who had robbed some houses and decided to rob the pond's bank, but they got into an argument during the robbery. Suddenly...the pond sloshed its icy cold water all over the men. In shock they ran downhill toward the mouth of the pond. To their amazement the pond opened its mouth and said, "I'll give you a head start to that tree over there and then I'll be after you." Hearing a voice come out of the mouth of the pond made them run even faster.

Nobody knew that the pond could also walk, and when the pond stood up with its fish, frogs, and cat-tails showing and walked after the robbers everyone looked at the pond in astonishment and said, "What are you doing?" The pond didn't stop to tell them, since it was obvious.

The little stream that ran out of the pond's mouth ran after the pond as he chased the robbers. The pond soon caught the robbers, who by now were so scared that they began looking for a jail just to get away from the walking and talking pond and the stream running out of its mouth. When the pond grabbed the robbers they nearly drowned and they were so cold and wet by the time they were put in jail that they built a fire to warm up and dry out. The jail soon caught on fire but luckily the pond was still nearby and put out the fire by just standing on it. The only trouble now was that he flooded the jail, but all the prisoners got a bath. He then decided he better walk home and become a normal pond again.

This type of project cultivates the creative image in chil-dren by taking them step-by-step through the creative process, while also producing a tangible result. But they don't have to come up with the first (or even their umpteenth) story by themselves—we can find a good book that's on their level and let them copy it. Educator and author Dr. Ruth Beechick recommends copying the work of a master as one way to develop the creative image of a child. Teachers used this approach during the Renaissance—art students in particular spent years copying the compositional techniques and brush strokes of the great masters. Technique and skill taught in this context develop taste, appreciation, and a vision for excellence. The best way to excel in any endeavor is to be mentored by masters, whether personally or through study of their great works.

> The best way to
> excel in any endeavor
> is to be mentored
> by masters.

## ENCOURAGING CREATIVE PLAY

Play is a state in which a child (or a childlike adult) is unselfconscious—completely enthralled. Energy flows. The body, the emotions, and the intellect are all coherently focused, driven by burning curiosity and caught up in the mystery of what's going to happen next. Play is an egoless state, since there's no risk or possibility of failure and judgment. In this state, creativity flourishes.

In *Hearth and Home,* Karey said, "I believe children need long stretches of time to complete their 'play thoughts.' They need the free time to pursue and perfect them. Children at play have a concentration analogous to the concentration of an artist and sometimes this 'play' needs time to develop and come full circle, but we so often disrupt them for running here and there and they lose this concentration and with continual disruptions they may even lose the ability to play."[62]

When children play, they exercise the creative image of God in themselves in the most natural way. Their creations will give us clues as to where their talents lie. When we've zeroed in on a talent, we can provide a child with tools to pursue that interest. Recently, I remodeled our older children's playhouse into a museum and lab for Dawson, since that's the area in which his creative imagination lies. It's where he plays. This is his workplace and his creating place.

Through the years, our children have been perpetually in the process of planning, designing, building, making. They inspired the line from the song I quoted at the end of the last chapter: "His goal's in the making, the building, creating...and not in what's finished and done." Children engaged in these activities are truly alive, because they're telling their story in the present—the only point where anyone, young or old, touches eternity.

Travis designed and assembled an electronic combination lock for his bedroom door from paper clips, brads, and disassembled appliances. He also designed and built an extensive underground fort, and a log cabin with a loft and a shake roof. He animated cartoons on his computer using software that would be considered primitive today.

For Heather, our house became the United States, and various rooms were regions or states where she took journeys with her Matchbox cars. She imagined that clouds hug mountains and wash them clean—which isn't far from the truth—and she loved to sit in the driver's seat of vehicles for hours, pretending she was driving.

Dawson's creations are in progress as I write this. Day after day, from morning to night, he's in nonstop motion like a busy beaver, making or planning something—except when he's sick. When he was seven years old, he caught a flu bug and ended up with an ear infection that kept him in the house for over a week. During that time he slipped a note to me:

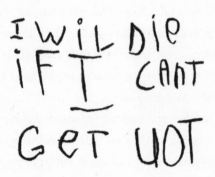

His frustration wasn't from squelched garden-variety hyperactivity. The creative image of God in Dawson demands physical expression.

Over the past several years, Dawson has made an oven out of bricks and mud, a six-foot-long swing that you lie down on as you swing, and a thirty-five-foot-long daisy chain to decorate our porch. He made a major addition to Travis's underground fort, complete with architectural plans and a scale model, and he created a city of three billion people on his SimCity computer program. We've responded to all of these projects with enthusiasm, acknowledging the ideas and encouraging the children to continue by supplying them with tools and time to create more things.

My friend Jim has never really known where his play ends and his work begins. He lives in the old mining town of Victor, Colorado, and is one of the most gifted people I know.

Though he never went to college, he received an honorary doctorate from a college for a paper he presented. He's an expert in all aspects of mining—from drilling to handling explosives to assaying the ore—a master mechanic and electrician, a theologian and inventor, and he has served his little town as mayor while also serving his church as pastor. Jim remembers a very real burning desire in his heart to design and build from about age three, when he built ramps so he could steal the sap from his father's maple sugaring buckets in the spring in New Hampshire.

By age five, Jim was building go-carts, racing them with no brakes or steering, until they disintegrated against a tree—usually with him driving—or just fell apart. When he was about seven, he moved to bigger things—getting under the hood of his father's DeSoto one day. Before he knew it, Jim had taken the thing half apart. He intended to put it back together—except he couldn't precisely recall which wires had been connected where. You can imagine his father's surprise when the car wouldn't start.

Not long afterwards, Jim constructed a helicopter from scrap lumber, with a rope and pulley to spin the propeller, hooked up to an electric motor. He fully expected the contraption to fly. His father just smiled as he plugged in the extension cord for Jim, with the words, "Hold on. Don't let it get away from you!"

Years later, Jim designed a single-person helicopter propelled by hydrogen peroxide, and this one flew. I'm not kidding. There's a video to prove it. The only thing that killed production was that his investors backed out when the stock market crashed in 1987.

Shortly after that, Jim got into gold mining, and he's been at it ever since, not to become wealthy but to support the work of missionaries and pastors around the world.

## SUPPORTING EARLY PASSION AND OLDER DESIRE

My dad was an exceptional baseball player in his youth, so he expected me to excel in the sport, starting with Little League. A number of problems interfered, the first being my exclusion by the locals because my religion was different from theirs. And although I was a good pitcher, I could never learn to hit the ball well. I could see the pitcher's release, but by the time the ball was near the plate it had become a blur that then disappeared.

Football was out, as my parents wanted to protect my knees. I tried running cross-country but was plagued with side cramps. At one meet, I came in second to last out of three hundred and fifty-seven runners—the only guy I beat broke his leg during the race.

Then I tried basketball. A young coach stuck me into a varsity game during my sophomore year in high school, and to everyone's surprise, I scored eleven points and pulled down an unusually high number of rebounds. "Coach" believed in me, and this had a major impact on my high school years and beyond. I began training year-round.

Mom and Dad gave me their complete support. They sent me to basketball camps they couldn't really afford. And Dad helped me build a basketball court in our backyard after I shared my dream of having a regulation court, totally to spec, so that when I played in the gym, it would be exactly the same.

At his insistence, I hand-dug two feet down through clay soil for the foundation of the asphalt pad he poured. This took weeks of backbreaking work, hauling the dirt away with a wheelbarrow. The court was equipped with lights and an official backboard and rim that hung ten feet out from the vertical support—a classy derricklike structure Dad designed. Our team practiced there all summer long. In the winter, I practiced wearing fingerless gloves, shooting a hundred free throws every day along with about the same number of jump shots.

"Coach" called me recently. We'd lost touch and hadn't talked for many years. He said, "It's kind of funny that when we're back in the Milwaukee area and I go past your old home, I check to see if you guys are shooting baskets in the backyard." The romance is mutual, and the faith invested in a child or young person can bring lifelong dividends—a truth wonderfully illustrated in the film *Mr. Holland's Opus.*

> *There's strong evidence that later childhood—from ten to fourteen—is the more natural time for the creative image of God to be manifest.*

It isn't uncommon for children even as young as five to express the specifics of their creative image. Their innate creative talent often comes with an uncommon passion for exercising and pursuing it, as though they know intuitively this is how God has designed them. During these early experimental years, parents should respond with support and encouragement—tempered with caution—plus wisdom, since each child's script is unique.

The lives of gifted individuals who were child prodigies often are characterized by burnout related to the loss of childhood and a loss of balance. Parents may make matters worse by trying to push, manage, or control such a child, but I'm careful not to condemn, for who knows how to parent such talent?

However, there's strong evidence that later childhood—from ten to fourteen—is the more natural time for the creative image of God to be manifest. A significant number of great musicians, especially violinists, began lessons at about this age. This may be the ideal time to get serious about helping our children define their specific creative image. By that time we hope they've grown strong from a healthy, diversified childhood, and the world is just beginning to come into cognitive focus. Regimented training, lessons, goals, and practice are much more appropriate for an emotionally and mentally competent child of fourteen than for a five-year-old.

The primary expression of their creative image may not occur until age eighteen to twenty-four. Even then, it may evolve over time. Grandma Moses began painting at seventy-six and continued until her death at one hundred and one. She never had an art lesson. I wrote my first legitimate song when I was forty-five. A friend of mine didn't start climbing mountains until he was in his late seventies. He had a heart attack in his sixties, and had never been athletic before then. Once, when I was out hiking with friends, all of us under full packs, we met him seven miles from the trailhead at ten thousand feet. He was in his mid-eighties by then, "just out for an afternoon stroll" without a backpack or canteen—just his necessary pills in his pocket.

These stories should inspire us by dissolving the illusion that the creative part of life is available only to the young or to those with special credentials in a specific creative area.

My friend Kathy is one of the most amazing women I know. The creative image of God in her was first manifested in her relationship with peers when she was a child. She always ended up in charge—the leader and problem solver. Kathy received Christ as her personal Savior when she was a child. From the start, it was apparent she wouldn't be successful in school. Due to complex eye problems and symptoms of attention deficit disorder, she struggled with academics, and her leadership ability went unrecognized. Fortunately, when she was just a little girl, her father told her, "Kathy, you can do anything you put your heart to." But because of her failure in school she began associating with the wrong crowd, which led her down a pathway to heartache.

With no education or training, a failed teenage marriage, and enough drama to fill several novels, this single mother then struggled with alcoholism, drugs, and poverty. When she had sunk to a point of desperation, she cried out to God, who at that moment miraculously reached down and saved her life. She asked God never to let her forget what she'd gone through, so she would always be sensitive to others. By sheer determination she started a dress shop business, which was successful. The creative image of God—stymied in her youth—was reappearing.

Then her second husband's brother and partner was killed in an auto accident, putting their company in crisis. After much discussion, Kathy was asked to come in and help out. With a national recession, and the company deep in debt,

Kathy—at age forty-two—took on the task of learning all she could in applications of fire-rated commercial construction. When she began she had no idea what spray fireproofing was, other than something she continually had to wash out of her husband's clothes.

Against all odds—including being a woman in an all-male field—she obtained a commercial contractor's license, pulled the company out of debt, and built it into the largest and most successful specialty subcontractor in its field in the country, and possibly the world. Beyond managing several companies, industrial park development, and a golf course, she's busy now with national trade organizations, and lobby and code bodies. She sits on several boards and chaired the committee that wrote the standard manual of practice for firestop installations.

How in the world did she do this? She says, "It was only through God's grace and my father's belief in me." She discovered inside herself a brilliant business sense and executive mind, an insatiable desire and ability to solve problems and bring order from disorder, and a unique entrepreneurial spirit that inspires all around her. This is the creative image of God in Kathy. It first showed itself when she was a child and, against tremendous odds, it survived and developed within her over time—an irresistible force set free to create. "No one," she says, "taught me to do what I do—I just do it." The plot of her story is familiar and never fails to inspire. I believe the key ingredient is the creative image of God. Although she could now retire, she's most happy and satisfied meeting challenges, solving problems, and leading the company.

If we want to help our children, as Kathy's father encouraged her, we need to let them know we believe in them. This single inner conviction—"My dad (or my mom) believes in me"—will do more to protect and nurture the creative image of God in a child than anything else, even if our encouragement takes years to bear fruit.

# Chapter 13

# Creative Domains

*It seems like just yesterday he stood at my knee.*
*His little fingers tuned my guitar.*
*He looked up at me with those big brown eyes,*
*And strummed me his first little tune.*

"DADDY, WHAT IS HER NAME?"

At seven years of age, Ben had never seen an artist's picture until he made one himself. He was born into the eighteenth-century Quaker faith, which frowned on "needless gaudy images." But this ordinary Quaker lad suddenly developed a strange urge and a stranger gift for drawing pictures. With a goose-quill pen and black ink, he drew a portrait of his sleeping baby sister, which his mother discovered. She said, "Memories grow old, but this picture of my darling will hold the memory." However, she didn't show the picture to Ben's father for a time.

Ben grew tired of only black ink, so one day his Native American friends taught him how to make colored paint from the earth. Still, he had no paintbrush. So the budding artist made his own paintbrush from hair clipped from his cat, Grimalkin. Within a few weeks the family began to notice the cat's deteriorating condition, so one night during family prayer time Ben's father prayed for poor Grimalkin, who was losing his hair.

254 Monte Swan

Ben then confessed. He showed his pictures to his father, who said, "Tell me why it is that thee must draw?" Ben was at a loss. How could he explain the need for putting things on paper? How could he explain how his fingers ached to draw? With reservation, his father gave him permission to continue his painting when he wasn't doing chores—which was rare. His father believed the boy would outgrow this fancy.

Eventually, however, Ben's father acknowledged his son's special gift, and the church elders gave the lad their consent to pursue painting instead of a "useful craft." Ben received a scholarship from an art academy in Philadelphia and went on to become "the father of American painting." He was also the only American to become the president of the English Royal Academy of Arts. Even as an aged man, Benjamin West spoke nostalgically of the cat that had been the constant companion of his boyhood and supplied him with hair for his first paint-brushes. You can read his story—one of my kids' favorites—in *Benjamin West and His Cat Grimalkin* by Marguerite Henry and illustrated by Wesley Dennis.

> *Creativity is actually a way of thinking, or even a way of living.*

Creativity spans a broad spectrum. It's actually a way of thinking, or even a way of living—so the creative image of God may find expression in any number of arenas. Mihaly Csikszentmihalyi refers to these arenas as "domains," which include art, baking, calligraphy, canoeing, computers, conversation, cooking, dancing, decorating, fencing, fly-fishing, flying model airplanes, football, forestry, gardening, mechanics, music, polo, publishing, reading, skiing, teaching, and tennis. Each domain has its own special rules, skills, knowledge, boundaries, and procedures.

Too often, we assume that most domains are off-limits. This habit of thought is frequently established during childhood, and has stifled and impoverished many lives. However, the creative urge is strong in children. Like steam in a boiling kettle, it will find a way to express itself, even in the face of withering suppression—not out of defiance, but out of deference to the One whose Spirit is empowering the child in question.

Benjamin West's creative domain was obviously painting. For many, their creative domain starts as an interest, develops into a hobby, then becomes an avocation that blossoms and bears fruit as a lifelong vocation. I love that word, vocation, because it means "calling," which is the whole point I'm trying to make. God calls each of us to fulfill some purpose in life. His calling is consistent with the creative image of Himself in us, which is most effectively exercised within a particular creative domain.

## DISCERNING CREATIVE DOMAINS

My mother not only studied my brothers and me, she acted on what she learned, using her creativity to win our hearts. One thing she did was teach her boys how to cook—in her own kitchen! And she laughed, rather than scolded, at the horrendous messes we made. My favorite creation was a variation on sponge candy, made by cooking down corn syrup and sugar with a little vinegar, until the mixture becomes brittle when dropped into cold water. The fun starts when you add in a little baking soda, and the candy erupts from the bowl like golden lava. I think my fascination with magma and volatiles started in Mom's kitchen, and it eventually led me to cofound a geologic company called MagmaChem.

My parents provided exposure to a wide range of activities chosen to harness the talents and energy they saw in me. And they kept trying, regardless of the financial and personal sacrifices required, so I could discover and develop my particular creative domains.

We can help our children discover their creative domains by exposing them to a variety of arenas in which creativity is required. The key here is broad exposure. To specialize and focus on one area too soon may overlook the child's primary area of creativity, and may throw them out of balance. But at some point it will be time to zero in on at least one domain. The most challenging part is keeping abreast of the changing abilities and desires of a growing child. It's like shooting at a moving target, since creativity is by nature dynamic.

Unusual talents, gifts, and abilities are not prerequisites for creativity. Not every child is a prodigy—the script God writes for each person is revealed only as it's lived. We just need to protect and cultivate the qualities necessary for creativity, which are innate in most children—a keen curiosity about their surroundings, awe about the mysteries of life, and an insatiable passion to solve them.

There's a story of a famous scientist who was walking in the woods as a youth when he noticed a large beetle scurrying under the bark of a tree. Because he didn't have this beetle in his collection, he ran to the tree, peeled off the bark, and grabbed the insect. That's when he saw two more. He wanted to collect these, too, but they were so large he could hold only one in each hand. In desperation, he popped the third beetle in his mouth and ran all the way home, trying to keep it from escaping down his throat!

A truly creative person will endure almost anything for the pure joy of pursuing and developing their particular bent, which ultimately finds expression in the same way water from an underground thermal always finds its way to the surface. For such people, none of the endeavor is work, no matter how challenging; it's all recreation in the truest sense of the word— "re-creation." Some would even call it play.

My friend Dave, who helped me write this book, shared with me how, at age eight, he borrowed some of his father's mimeo cushion sheets and produced a little newspaper, which he peddled around the neighborhood. In his mind, he's always been a writer. Creatively speaking, he looked in the mirror when he was eight and saw not a child, but a writer. Gazing back at him was not a third-grader missing a couple of teeth, but the creative image of God. It was almost as if he had met his own soul and discovered his destiny. He knew who he was, and that writing would be his way of cocreating with the One who had created him.

Today, Dave edits a major Christian medical magazine and has produced eleven books, including this one. As we work together, it's obvious he has a gift. I feel God's image in him as he wades through my manuscripts, straightening out the logical flow and helping me find the right words. He knows the truth of Mark Twain's oft-quoted statement equating the difference between the right word and the almost-right word with the difference between lightning and a lightning bug.

## FACILITATING THE PROCESS

Mom is an excellent pianist, so when I was in junior high she enrolled me in piano lessons for several months. It soon became obvious I wasn't programmed for the keyboard. But studying music led me to the trumpet, which I loved. My parents bought me a quality instrument and arranged for lessons with a professional jazz musician. Later, they transported me many miles weekly so I could study with a concert trumpet player. My goal was to become a professional trumpet player, until I had an allergic reaction to the metal of the mouthpiece and was forced to quit playing.

At about the same age, I started wood carving. My parents bought me *How to Do Wood Carving*, by John Lacey. Now, as I thumb through its yellowed pages, the old-book smell and finger smudges connect me with a wonderful boyhood of whittling. My parents equipped me with German-made knives and quality pieces of wood. First I used pine, but I soon advanced to hardwoods—my favorites being walnut and maple. I still love the smell of freshly sanded walnut. I carved in my bedroom, on the workbench Dad had built, taking as long as three days to make a whitetail deer. My hobby produced piles of wood chips and sawdust that I tracked all over the house. Mom and Dad ignored the mess, which they knew was temporary, and focused instead on my creations—and my creativity, which they knew would be a lifelong pursuit. Their encouragement and praise taught me to do the same for my own children, and now I smile when I find wood chips leading from all parts of the house to Dawson's bedroom.

We can easily miss this process of discovery and growth in

our own child if we're constantly distracted by matters of lesser importance—such as paying the mortgage, advancing a career, attending committee meetings, or keeping the floors spotless. Worse, we can put out the fire by critiquing instead of encouraging, or by dictating instead of enjoying the script.

In the film *Dead Poets Society,* a young man with a passion and gift for acting is denied the opportunity to pursue his dreams by his father, who insists he must

> *We can put out the fire by critiquing instead of encouraging, or by dictating instead of enjoying the script.*

go to medical school. The boy commits suicide, because he cannot live within the script his father has written for him. This character was an adolescent, but when younger children are controlled by their parents in the same way, denied the opportunity to explore their creative domains, they die inside.

Our role as parents is to facilitate. It is God who is at work in our child, "both to will and to do for His good pleasure" (Philippians 2:13). Hindering His will and work dishonors God, who has gifted our child in a particular, unique way. We must not limit them to what we can imagine, but try to discover their passions and follow where they lead. If we don't, they'll become discouraged. If, through God's grace, they do develop a creative domain without our help, we'll have forfeited the great joy of romancing them through our relationship.

Alan, a master mechanic who grew up in New Hampshire, lives near us. He's the son of a minister who comes from a long family tradition of ministers and missionaries, so people probably assumed he would also "go into the ministry." But from a very early age, Alan's joy was taking things apart and putting them back together. Since this wasn't up his father's alley, his father more or less ignored Alan's interests in favor of tending his "flock." So Alan built models, moved on to cars, then to bigger things—much bigger, as in the Air Force—before settling back to maintaining our county's vehicles, which includes fixing snowplows on snowy nights. He hasn't gone into the ministry officially, but he does have a ministry, one I believe is even more dynamic than many official ministries. He's out in the midst of the battle, caring for the wounded and lost. He works with widows, single moms, and hurting people, repairing their vehicles for little or no pay. Like an old-fashioned doctor, he makes house calls. Alan is, therefore, a minister, even though he wields the tools of a mechanic.

When we consider our child's creative image and the domains in which it might be best expressed, we should try to see the horizon of possibilities as broadly as God sees them. Just as the body needs all its parts, so the body of Christ, of which we adults and children are members, needs all of God's creative gifts given to function most effectively (1 Corinthians 12–14). Not everyone can be a painter, poet, politician, or pastor. We all have lofty dreams for our children; the crucial issue isn't our dreams, but theirs. More important is God's vision for their creative role in His Story. Mechanic or missionary or both, it's His calling that counts.

## DEVELOPING CREATIVE DOMAINS

A child needs our help to develop skills, abilities, and talents in a particular creative domain. We should provide proper equipment and seek out coaches or mentors. Creative domains are found in work and play, vocation and recreation, occupation and hobby, career and ministry.

During the ten years that I roamed the western United States as a young geologist, I was reading the story God had written in the rocks and getting paid to do so. The little boy in me who had hugged the pine stump was now completely immersed in God's creation—enchanted, spellbound, captivated by the Lord's continuing romance of my heart. This happened because my parents had released me, with no strings attached, to follow my calling.

Ideally, the creative image of God should be expressed in our life's work. If it is, work will be more enjoyable and successful because our heart as well as our talents will naturally be in it. Some creative interests that could potentially become our work develop early in childhood, but most, as I've suggested, develop between ten and fourteen years of age. This is when we as parents should consider making it a point to arrange a variety of trial flights from the "nest" for our children, in the company of trusted mentors who will teach, guide, and befriend them.

But first, we must know the passions of our child. Second, we need to find a Christian older than our child, usually an adult, who shares one of their passions and has time to be a kindred spirit. This could be a plumber, musician, doctor, rancher, computer engineer, carpenter, or homemaker. If we can show our children someone who's "cool" and who also embraces our values, principles, and beliefs, this will both draw and woo their hearts, and reinforce our training.

Our daughter, Heather, seems to have found her niche,

after help from several wonderful mentors. She attended a community college and a Bible college, and graduated from a culinary arts school. Her vision was to work in the hospitality industry on dude ranches and camps. Reality, however, turned out to be not exactly consistent with what she had pictured.

First, the food was seldom made from scratch. In some cases it was trucked in, precooked and frozen. Heather has learned home-style and gourmet cooking from Karey—she even grinds her own flour. The other surprise was the multi-tasked, high-pressure working environment. Most head cooks are unusual women—they probably could have been CEOs or drill sergeants, had they wished. Heather is sweet and gentle, and this wasn't a good fit.

Along the way, several women who had mentored Heather in a variety of arenas all said—more than once—that Heather's gifts are special, ideally suited for working with children or the elderly. I believe they were seeing the creative image of God in Heather. Through following their counsel, Heather began her work at a life-care center. Her Mother Teresa–like bedside manner, sweet smile, and gentle

> *The key for mentors is that they view what they do as a calling and are excited and passionate about it.*

personality are a huge hit with the residents. They naturally confide in her. Consequently, she shares Christ with them in the same way a chaplain would, with gentle compassion. She has told us it feels so good to have found her place of work and ministry. Her mentors were instrumental in this process.

The youth subculture competes determinedly for the hearts of our children. Many parents have felt this competitive wedge being driven between them and their children. By contrast, mentors who are kindred spirits and have childlike hearts give our children a genuine alternative.

It's a mentor's responsibility to walk alongside and pass on knowledge and skills, while romancing the child to God through the shared experience. The key is that they view what they do as a calling and are excited and passionate about it.

Travis began working with an inventor when he was thirteen. This person inspired Travis's heart and opened up the world of small business and risk taking to him. To Travis's surprise and delight, his mentor also had a wonderful sense of humor. At age fifteen, Travis was the youngest senators' aide working in the state capitol. Through this experience, he learned much about protocol and the legislative process, as well as how to feel comfortable wearing a suit.

For several years, Travis worked with a Denver University professor and his entrepreneurial son, manufacturing microdissection surgical needles. Daily exposure to the adult culture was valuable, as were the research and problem-solving skills he acquired. He also joined a small worship band at a local weekly youth gathering when he turned sixteen. The worship leader trained Travis in the basics of worship leading, and he discovered that he had leadership and musical production gifts. Now, while still in college, Travis has been the worship leader for a large church on campus, and it appears that "worship minister" may be his vocation.

When he was in senior high, Travis gave a presentation during a workshop at an educational conference. Part of his speech went like this:

Most high schoolers think of their first job as just a way to make some extra spending money. They typically end up flipping hamburgers with like-minded high schoolers at the local fast food establishment. It is not that this is an undesirable job, but few high schoolers will ever own a fast food restaurant. For me, the workplace is more than just a place for making money—it is a laboratory where I test my talents and education, and gain real-life knowledge and experience working with adults who do what I think I might like to do for my life's work. If you can't find a paying job, find a volunteer position doing something you are interested in. Don't worry about the pay. In a short time, if you do a good job, chances are that they will begin paying you anyway. It's a great way to find a high-quality job and build a résumé of experience. I know, because it happened to me.

## COMMON DOMAINS—THREE EXAMPLES

### 1. Competitive Sports

Our culture is obsessed with competitive sports and athletics—and some of the reasons are valid. Sports develop teamwork, discipline, leadership skills, character, and healthy bodies. From personal experience I've tasted the challenge, the joy, the pain, and the glory because I ate, drank, and slept basketball for seven straight years. When I gave it up, it took me months to reequilibrate emotionally. Was I out of balance? Yes and no.

Balance is a complex concept. Great feats and defining moments in history are generally not thought of as products of balance. In fact, balance is generally considered a rather boring concept. But it's not! Balance is a dynamic state of perpetual moving, compensating, calculating, shifting—in a sense it's like a dance. If we try walking across a rushing river on a narrow log, we'll find that balance is both an exciting athletic challenge and a test of intellect, emotions, and character.

Balance depends on our most deeply held values and vision, which provide our frame of reference and plumb line. Without them, balance is impossible. When I ate, drank, and slept basketball, I was actually in balance with my deepest desires and dreams. If I'd known then that archery, music, and writing would one day be my passions, then my frame of reference would have been different, and the way I balanced everything would also have been different.

What's the purpose and objective of sports in our child's life? Are these consistent with our child's values and vision, and with ours? Is our focus long- or short-term? Some athletic activities can be enjoyed only when a person is young. Should we allow children to sacrifice their knees for a few short years of pleasure and glory, and the opportunity to develop specific character traits and a strong, coordinated body? Or do we help them preserve their knees for a full life of other physical pursuits, without the strength that early years of competitive sports develop? Do we encourage our children to invest their young lives in a lifelong sport such as golf, or a temporary sport such as gymnastics? Should they learn how to ski or

> *Balance depends on our most deeply held values and vision.*

how to tackle a quarterback? How to ride a bull or a bicycle? Are individual sports a better lifelong investment than team sports? Or do we want our child to do them all?

These questions need to be handled with care. Every child is unique, and there's no simple formula. Their interests may change from week to week, day to day, or even from moment to moment—which means we must keep an open mind about any sports commitment. In an earlier chapter, I mentioned my friend Ray. He and his wife, Trish, have five children—four boys and a girl. Trish told me how their family has flexed with the interests of each:

We have always felt it was crucial to expose each of our kids to various athletic experiences. Since the first three children were boys, the fall sport activity of choice was soccer. When nearly four seasons had gone by, our youngest, Caroline, made her debut on the four-to-six-year-old team with her brother, Patrick. One game into the season, her desire to play soccer seemed to wane. She had been in the game only a short time when she said, "Mommy, please take me out of here. I don't like soccer."

Since I was the coach, I said, "Well then, just hang out with Mommy." She preferred sitting on the sidelines, either coloring or playing dolls. Since we like to take videos of all our kids, we begged her to just go in for one minute, so Daddy could get a little footage. The big moment came and the footage Ray took is a treasure. Every time the ball rolled toward her, Caroline ran in the other direction. When it was kicked toward her, she bent down and covered her head with her hands. As she came out of the game, her comment was, "Mommy, can I try ballet instead?"

Now, two years later, ballet, gymnastics, swimming, and tennis have all been part of Caroline's sporting activities. She has had a great deal of enthusiasm for each of these and has commented that she might even try soccer once more. Exposure and variety have been keys in our children's development—always having an open mind and never closing doors. Development involves a complex and dynamic interplay of motor and cognitive skills, as well as success and failure. This makes our children physically, emotionally, and spiritually well-rounded.

Caroline still is our precious princess, as the only girl among four brothers. She continues to prefer dolls, dress up, and ballet, but she steps up to all the challenges we hand her and completes the tasks whether they're her "bag" or not. She is God's wonderful, unique creature, so we look forward to seeing what she may become.

## 2. The Fine Arts

Our children need to experience personally the texture, colors, and hues of original paintings. The brush strokes of the artist speak volumes that are lost in reproduction, as do the grand scale of the canvases of the masters. These firsthand experiences allow us to sense and witness the creative image of the artist, which may connect on a soul mate level with God's creative image in our children.

A friend and watercolor artist, Beth Thurow, once wrote:

The brain's tools are language, intelligence, reason, and creativity (ability to be innovative with principles). These, combined with conscience, free will, emotion, and self-awareness, define the human soul. Some paintings may be intellectual exercises, others driven by sheer emotion. Nevertheless, whether profound or silly, your state of soul meets the artist's at the art piece. If two souls sublimely agree, then Emmanuel (God with us) can incarnate. We weep.[63]

Involvement in the arts is often considered purely a leisure activity, frivolous and entertaining, but not practical. This attitude misses the point of God's creative image within us. God created because it brought Him joy. We create because He made us like Himself. Too often, modern "Christian" artists create their works out of good intentions, around sermonettes and the retelling of Bible stories. Their creations carry meaning in concrete, not abstract, form. A non-Christian would label it propaganda.

Where's the soul of the artist in Christian "elevator music" or in the knickknacks cramming the shelves of Christian bookstores? As secular investors control more and more of the business that has grown up around Christian "art," its soul seems to be further impoverished. Perhaps our children will help to change all this. But only if we support them, the way my parents supported me.

After high school I played two years of college basketball before the first injury of my career changed my life forever.

Since I was laid up, I accepted an invitation to a ski retreat, during which I found myself at a table in a ski lodge with thirty-six girls—all beautiful! One of the girls was leading songs on her guitar. I hadn't sung since sixth grade, which had been a disaster because my voice was changing and music was just not cool then. The girls forced me to sing, and to my complete surprise I could. As a result, a whole new nonathletic world opened up. The next week, a guy in our dorm gave me a beat-up old guitar. Within a couple of hours I was playing and singing "They Call the Wind Mariah." That day, my passion for basketball began transferring to music, and in my junior year I dropped out of basketball to pursue music.

My parents were completely shocked when I broke the news, since it was a major change in direction. But after talking it over, they supported me. They recognized that this change reflected my heart. The next time I came home they bought me a good guitar.

Soon I started a singing group called The Damascus Road. Our aim was to give churches a fresh vision for youth ministry. I enlisted college students as speakers and we had minicrusades. It was a stretch for me to be on stage in a nonbasketball mode, but it turned out to be preparation for future ministry. Along the way the members of our group taught me music.

I think my parents adapted so well to this new direction because they had no agenda of their own for me. For years they'd been praying this simple prayer: "Dear Lord: Grant our sons common sense, good judgment, and wisdom." As a result, they trusted me (or maybe they trusted God more!). During all my decision-making at that time, I never forgot my parents' trust and I did my best to be worthy of it. It gave me hope that everything was going to work out. And hope, at that point, was as vital to me as air, food, and water.

Through the years, another key to the development of my music ministry has been the encouragement of others who believed in me. I hesitate to think of where I'd be with music, had it not been for several church music ministers who mentored me, sharing and challenging me with their vision for music's role in addressing the needs of the church at any given time. They asked me to create. They were catalysts who stimulated me to produce musical dramas, original songs, and stage sets used in ministry with them. Nearly all my creative works can be traced back to a person's act of trust in me.

> For years my parents prayed, "Dear Lord: Grant our sons common sense, good judgment, and wisdom."

Music, a vital creative domain, is all around us. It has become the background static of life—the radio, boom boxes, phones, Walkman radios, in doctors' offices, in movies, everywhere. Teenagers listen to music at least half the hours they're awake. There's no doubt music stands apart from the other arts. Its power penetrates the heart, striking it directly with a message—whether truth or lie. Often its message is not in propositional form. It's incarnate in the rhythm and the harmony. It tells a story in a language that immediately communicates a message to our souls. How it does this is a mystery.

Karey and I have recorded several albums. Our experience has been that exposing our children to good music early, when their ears were still sensitive and life was relatively quiet, was key to helping them know what we value and treasure. Contemporary music that's complex to the point of sounding chaotic to young ears, with an unresolved structure and message, can overwhelm, destabilize, and confuse children. There's also a danger of addiction to some forms, not to mention possible evil that can seep into their minds through their ears. Music ultimately is an expression of the heart of the music's creator. I believe it's bordering on abuse to bring disharmony and despair into a child's life through music.

Listening is wonderful, but making our own music is even more wonderful. Music lessons are a part of many parents' strategies. A host of variables must be considered, including the child's talent, age, musical desire, and the practicality of a particular instrument—for instance, tuba versus guitar. Our pastor, Peter Hiett, accurately expresses the feelings of many of us adults as we look back on our own childhood music lesson experiences. "I quit because none of my enlightened friends in third grade thought piano was cool. And, to be honest, I'd never listened to any great piano music."

I believe maintaining strict control of our children's music as they move into their teen years is misguided. Some children are gifted with an ear that comprehends complex music that to a less gifted parent's ear is noise. Of course a line must be drawn at the point where chaos, evil, and destruction enter in. There will always be debate about where we draw the line, but there is a line. In only a few short years our teenagers will be totally free to choose their own music. Communicating to them, while they're still at home, that we respect their freedom to choose and their personal opinion and taste, and even trust their judgment, places the responsibility on their shoulders, and makes them more apt to listen to us. Open communication, sharing our perspective and knowledge in a spirit of camaraderie, is our best hope. They will then be more inclined to do what's right—assuming they understand the difference between right and wrong in this context. Here's where earlier teaching and training pay off.

Plato said, "All learning which is required under compulsion has no hold upon the mind."[64] Battle lines drawn over music alienate children. Why are we battling anyway? We're supposed to be on the same team. Moral lectures and rigid rules can undo years of romancing, because values learned under compulsion have no hold on the heart.

Our best line of action is to expose our children early to good music, to develop their appreciation of it, and to help them develop a Christian worldview that will be reflected in their musical tastes. If we're students of our children, we can help them find the musical niche that fits best as we provide instruction in musical skills and techniques, and attend live performances together.

Karey's mother played classical music and opera, along with current popular adult music, when Karey was growing up. The music was simply there—no lectures, no talk, no expert commentary. Karey's current enjoyment of classical music (beyond her need for peace) is probably due to that exposure.

## 3. Computers and Related Technology

Computers have opened up an entirely new creative domain in the last generation—a literal "new age" that still makes some adults uncomfortable, while most kids jump in with both feet from day one. Computers are commonplace in American homes—some households have half a dozen. My brothers are all PC experts, while I just commune with my friendly Macintosh. My business partner, who's a great earth scientist, will hardly touch a computer. Karey's brother, a systems engineer, wields his with great skill.

Early in Travis's education, I asked several computer scientists for their advice regarding how to acquaint him with computers. They said typing skills are essential and should be taught early (eight to twelve years of age). They also suggested I use computers as electronic "flash cards" for Travis's memory work. They said to wait until junior high before I introduced him to the more cognitive applications such as computer programming. This advice was consistent with the childhood development patterns I'd researched, so I took their advice. The results have been fascinating.

After years of typing training, Travis started, at age twelve, animating with the simple program HyperCard. He moved quickly into programming with BASIC. I remember buying FoxPro and arranging time for him with an accountant and a database manager, but that was a dead end, so I backed off. At fourteen, he worked for a small computer company where a couple of passionate entrepreneurial computer scientists provided opportunity for extensive hands-on experience with computer hardware. He took computers apart, cleaned and rebuilt them, and learned a wide range of practical skills in the process.

During this time, Travis literally grew up with the Internet, which in itself was a unique opportunity because he experienced history in the making. There were tense times when we knew he could get around any computer filter designed by man. It came down to a matter of trust. I prefer having the computer our children use be in a more open family room.

The FBI came knocking on our door looking for him one day, which sobered him up considerably. He hadn't done anything wrong, but he'd witnessed a hack and they wanted to know the details. He was amazed at how little they actually understood about the hacking world.

Eventually, Travis decided not to pursue computer science—the hardware, software writing, or networking career tracks. Instead, he chose art and computer graphic design. I've heard him use this analogy as an explanation: "Instead of designing, building, or servicing the vehicle, I wanted to drive it."

Although Travis is a Macintosh man, he serviced most of the PCs in his dorm at college—working on the hardware and software for the students, including helping computer science majors solve their computer-related problems. His broad understanding turned out to be unique among his classmates. His computer talent was obvious to us early on, so we opened many doors for him to walk through. Although most computer talent lands in software writing or networking, he took his talent into music and art, which, he has discovered, is not that common a combination.

Computers, related technology, and the Internet are a double-edged sword for our children. Though some Christians condemn these relatively new creative domains, I view them as more or less neutral. Yes, they can be addictive. Yes, a computer screen can have the same mesmerizing effect on a child as a television screen. Yes, there are dangers lurking around every corner on the Internet, from pornography to pedophiles. But for our children to function effectively in their new world, knowledge of computers and related technologies is essential. Common sense and open communication are keys to successfully guiding our children through this maze.

If our child expresses a creative interest, as Travis did, we can provide good equipment and programs, and connect them with trustworthy, like-minded mentors who can take them to the highest level possible. We cannot control completely what our son or daughter does with a computer when we aren't around. We need to give our fears to God, and to trust our children with this charge: "I'm allowing you access to this technology as my investment in your future. I'm not going to be looking over your shoulder or worrying every minute, because I trust you. I believe in you. And I know that when you encounter situations involving right and wrong, you'll try to choose wisely because you are who you are—not just my child, but a child of God, who will give you all the wisdom you need whenever you ask."

Every child is unique, and creativity by definition produces something novel and different. We should expect to break new ground with each of our children. As we do, we need to remember that God has placed some unique aspect of His creative image in every child, as if He'd implanted the score for an instrument in a cosmic symphony. Our role as parents is to

> *Creativity by definition produces something novel and different.*

help our children discover what part they're to play in this grand orchestra.

This flies in the face of the pressure for conformity that so often drives opinions and decisions in the Christian church today. When we play the wrong instrument or note, we're in discord and the symphony is out of tune. If God wants my son to be a choreographer, or your daughter to become a waste management engineer, it is to their own Master and yours—and not any modern-day pharisee—that we all must answer (Romans 14:4). The same goes for domains from sewing to surgery, pie making to photojournalism, homemaking to hockey, movie making to missionary medicine.

God didn't design us all to play the same note, nor does He desire for us to do so. He wants us to find our "instrument," develop our talents, discover the score, then make great music together with all the others who are following the right Conductor. There's a faint memory of the sound of the symphony within us all, and when we hear the music it brings joy. It's a celebration of truth and beauty, an echo of Eden and a prelude to the Master's piece.

Today, reading a good book and discussing it with Karey or the kids is every bit as exciting for me as basketball ever was. I feel the same way about communing with my friends about matters of mutual interest, from skiing to storytelling, eschatology to piscatology (my favorite is muskieology), ornithology, entomology, cooking, architecture, mechanics, mining, ministry, or making ice cream—whatever the topic of the moment may be. Although I still challenge myself with things such as pursuing elk in the mountains with a bow and arrow, or wild trout with a fly rod, hunting ideas and thoughts that lead me to God's truth is the creative domain that especially brings me joy these days.

After pursuing so many physical challenges throughout my life, it surprises and excites me to think I've never had more fun than during the creative journey that produced this book. It has been all the more enjoyable with the company and camaraderie of Dave Biebel, as we've worked through it word by word. Here I am in a whole new creative domain after passing age fifty. It makes me wonder what's next.

# High and Far

*With the bow bent, the arrow anchored,*
*We released our little boy,*
*Now he flies into his future,*
*To a place we may not see.*

"HIGH AND FAR"

E arly one spring day several years ago, a crew of concrete workers was pouring the walls for a root cellar under our kitchen. We live at an elevation of eight thousand feet, so there was still quite a bit of snow on the ground, but it was warm and sunny. The owner of the company had brought his little boy, Bronson, along. I was practicing shooting my bow in our meadow below our house when Bronson walked up to me and said, "Mr. Swan, will you teach me how to shoot a bow like you do?"

I said I'd love to, if he promised to work hard and listen to my instructions. With his father's permission, we began.

I led Bronson through all the steps—choosing a target, assuming the proper stance, gripping the bow, bending the bow arm slightly, nocking the arrow, using correct back tension. As I guided him, Bronson followed the steps until he was at full draw, ready to shoot his first arrow. He'd done everything perfectly and was intently focused on the target as I reminded him to think of one thing—aiming. I can still remember seeing his little fingers gripping the bowstring and his blue eyes riveted, with all the passion his ten-year-old heart could muster, on the bull's-eye.

Just as Bronson released his first arrow, we heard a swishing sound behind us. We turned to see a red plastic sled streaking down the hill with Dawson, then four years old, lying in it on his stomach with his head facing downhill. In that position, even had he known how to steer, steering would have been impossible. Dawson had just missed a fence post and a tree and was headed toward our wooden beehives and aspen grove. If he happened to miss the hives, there was no way he would miss the trees.

I dropped my bow and sprinted down the hill, mukluks and all. After a thirty-yard sprint I became Superman for a moment, diving through the air to catch the sled. With arms fully extended I was able to grab it by the left rear end, stopping Dawson one foot from the beehives. The snow cushioned my landing and I rolled to the side of the beehives with Dawson and the sled in hand.

Dawson tumbled out of the sled and turned over in the slushy spring snow. He sat up with a big smile, rosy cheeks shining with melting snow, and exclaimed, "Hey, Papa—that was fun! Let's do it again!" He'd enjoyed the ride more than anything because his papa had participated with such extravagant passion. I had not only jumped into Dawson's metaphorical mud puddle, I had rolled in it! But he remained oblivious to the danger and to the fact he'd aimed his sled in the wrong direction. On top of that, he had no idea he'd distracted Bronson.

Bronson was hanging his head in disappointment. His

arrow had missed the target, glanced off a tree, and careened end over end into an outcrop of granite, which abruptly ended its flight. As a result, the arrow's nock broke off, and the point was smashed and shoved up the shaft, which was bent. It was repairable but would be an inch shorter, scarred and dented, and never again truly straight.

He'd done everything right, except that he'd moved the bow before the arrow cleared the arrow rest. It takes only a split second for an arrow to be free of the string and the bow, but that last split second is critical to the success of the shot.

Psalm 127 says that our children are like arrows in our quiver, and for almost two decades that's where they stay as we prepare them to fly straight and true when they leave us.

## AIMING YOUR CHILDREN

As I began writing this epilogue, my mother called and shared with me this old letter she had recently come across. She and

dear Grandpa and Grandma

thank you for the jack knife.

thank you for thinking that i'm

old enough to have it I cut myself

3 time's.

Love

travis

Dad had just had a great laugh as they read it again.

For some parents, releasing a child into the world feels like handing them a knife before they're prepared to use it properly. We can become obsessed with the fear of little cuts, only to miss the essential truth that our children desperately desire and need our encouragement, belief, faith, and trust. Travis was thanking his grandma and grandpa for their trust in him. Through this simple gift they were helping me aim him in the right direction.

Like Travis, I also experienced their investment of trust in me. Trust usually is conditional, earned, or built on a history of behavior. But my parents' trust had an unconditional twist because they knew something about me that I didn't. Their trust gave me hope, and hope for a child is as vital as air, food, and water. If they believed in me, it was okay for me to believe in myself. Yes, I was being aimed—but with my informed consent. I wasn't coerced but inspired to find and fulfill my unique destiny as their child and God's.

A friend of mine told the story of a college student he was discipling. The young man had dabbled in drugs and had run around with the wrong crowd, but his heart now desired God. My friend asked him, "Why did you come back to God?"

The young man said, "When I was in high school, every morning my father, who you know is a high-powered businessman, drove me to school. And as I opened the car door he never failed to reach over, put his hand on my arm and say, 'Son, remember, I believe in you.' This one statement more than anything else kept me from getting into serious trouble. It has wooed me back to God. Those words haunted me as I strayed. They reached something deep inside me and called me to be better. I have finally begun living up to the faith my dad had in me. He saw something in me I didn't see—his son conformed to the image of Christ."

The way this father saw his son is parallel to the way God views all who trust in Christ for salvation—as already made perfect through His grace. He's saying, "I love you. And there's nothing you can ever do or say that will change that." The Greek root for belief simply means "to give one's heart to." This is how perfect love casts out fear—and the need to prove anything. The question for the child—whether in physical or spiritual terms—becomes: "How can I honor (and not disappoint) someone who has such faith in me?"

What if our child hasn't earned our trust, or has squandered it in the past? Trust may be conditional, but faith is not. This is risky, but it's also where grace comes in. A parent who has faith in a child who seems unworthy of trust may be surprised by the response. Of course there are no guarantees where humans are concerned. But I do know that conditional, controlling "love," which demands payment before it takes the risk of faith, will never succeed. Philip Yancey said, "Doubt always coexists with faith, for in the presence of certainty who would need faith at all?"[65] And Kathleen Norris shares this statement from a monk, "Doubt is merely the seed of faith, a sign that faith is alive and ready to grow."[66]

There's a fine line here between grace-filled faith and false faith. In either case, our approach to our child during the final phase of parenting clearly indicates whether we're involved in a romance, or a business venture. A parent who operates with bookkeeping logic is basically selfish—probably engaged in self-protection, which so often seems justified. After all, what will the neighbors, the larger family, or church members think of parents whose children seem to be crooked arrows?

Real love—the kind God expressed for us through Jesus—is risky and sometimes very costly. The apostle Paul wrote that love "bears all things, believes all things, hopes all things, endures all things" (1 Corinthians 13:7). In Matthew 25, where Jesus tells the parable of the talents (a unit of currency), I believe we find biblical support for investing faith (even as we doubt) in our child, in the form of unconditional grace.

In the parable, one servant didn't invest the talent given to him because he was afraid he might lose it. Instead, he hid the money in the ground. His lord called him a "wicked and lazy servant." This appears on the surface to be a somewhat harsh judgment for being conservative. But Jesus was saying that faithfulness requires using or investing what God entrusts to us, for His glory. Within the context of parenting, the "talent" entrusted to parents by the Lord is the faith we can either invest into or withhold from our children. To hold back is an act of self-protection motivated by fear and a lack of trust in God.

Larry Crabb has said that the sin of self-protection is very difficult to recognize, acknowledge, and deal with because change must come from the inside out.[67] Self-protection seems at face value justified, as in the case of the wicked and lazy servant. We don't want to play the fool, be disappointed, or have our investment in our children return void. The choice not to risk has a wise, frugal ring to it, which in another context might be noble. To react defensively when doubt arises seems—and may even be—rational. But to invest our faith unconditionally, even though the venture appears risky, is an act of courage and grace. Without an eternal perspective, this appears foolish, naive, and unwise. Supernatural logic always seems this way to the secular mind. But "the wisdom of this world is foolishness with God" (1 Corinthians 3:19).

Jesus gave His life for undeserving, wayward sinners—including us and our children—because He believed the will of His Father was good, and His Word trustworthy. Our Savior is our model. Incarnating His character is the central issue in properly aiming the arrows we hope will honor Him. By faith, we can proceed, trusting not in our own abilities or even in our children's character, but in Christ, who will persevere with them more than they with Him, or we with them. We can, therefore, release them with confidence, hope, and joy.

## RELEASING YOUR CHILDREN

Releasing—an arrow or a child—is not an event but a process involving a series of events. In archery, this series of events happens in the blink of an eye. In parenting the process is much longer, although when we look back it will seem to have been but the blink of the eye.

As our children near adulthood, they begin testing what we've taught them through the years. It's a suspenseful time for parents because everything is up in the air, pending our children's decisions. As Christians, we wonder if they'll make God the object of their passion. They stretch our patience and our finances, go on to college, or start a job. We wonder—even sometimes worry—about their careers, their calling, their future spouses, and as they become more independent we realize that soon they'll be completely on their own. It's natural for parents to become preoccupied with these events, sometimes forgetting how much of the process has already happened.

Recently, I spoke at a conference where a woman told me that she was at a loss as to what to do with her daughter, who was about to go away to college. She said, "Our relationship is crumbling. My daughter isn't in rebellion against God, but she's rebelling against me." This bewildered the mother, since her daughter had been a model child through her entire life, including high school.

"Give me an example of your conflict," I said.

"She won't keep her room clean," the distraught mother replied.

As far as I could see, the conflict was mostly inside the mother. But for her, the crisis was real and it was threatening to cause a major relational disaster. She was trying to stand by her principles, and the daughter was trying to make her own choices.

"Most eighteen-year-old females are preoccupied with major life changes and choices," I reminded her. "If ever you err on the side of grace it should be now."

"But she knows the rules," the mother said. "I feel that to change them just because she won't keep them anymore would violate everything I've taught her. And it would be a bad example for her younger sister. All we need is for the house to become a pigpen for the next three years."

Over several weeks of coaching by phone, I tried to encourage this mother to raise her sights. She was looking only at the daughter's newfound sloppiness. I encouraged her to try to look past the dirt to her daughter's heart. "In the process of releasing," I said, "we do best when we major in the majors and overlook the minors."

The lady was experiencing what archers call "target panic." At the instant the arrow is released, while the shaft is moving along the arrow rest, the archer flinches, deflecting the arrow, causing it to miss its mark. Target panic is responsible for up to 90 percent of misses under twenty-five yards in range, since most serious archers can become quite proficient up to that distance. Why this panic happens in a person normally confident in their aim is difficult to determine, because most archers with this problem blank out mentally and cannot recall the small details of what actually happened. The issue, as far as I can see, is again a matter of belief and faith, or trust. Even an archer with good form and good equipment properly set up can miss, if they allow fear, anxiety, or worry to creep in as distractions at the last split second. The strange thing is that, for most who experience target panic, the focus becomes the equipment or the setup, or too much or too little practice, when the remedy is faith that follows through, holding the bow steady until the arrow has completely cleared the bow.

## FOLLOWING THROUGH

Archers differ in their shooting styles. Some close an eye, some cant the bow, some use a mechanical release, and some use fingers to pull back the string. Anchor points and methods of gripping the handle vary. Some archers shoot with bent arm; others shoot straight-armed. Techniques vary in archery—as in parenting—but no archer or parent can hope to hit the target without proper follow-through.

As I finish this book, Travis is in his third year of college. He's still partly supported by us; he hasn't totally settled on a vocation, nor is he married. He doesn't own a house; he has told us his home is now at college. This arrow is pulling away from the bowstring. We spent a lot of time together as he was growing up. We homeschooled him all the way—even through high school. But I'm currently spending more time with him by phone and e-mail in heart-to-heart discussion about crucial issues and watershed decisions than I did at any time when he was home.

It isn't that I'm having a hard time letting go; we're simply close friends—best friends. It's a wonderful relationship. I often think of the words of young Teddy Roosevelt, who wrote to his father while attending Harvard, "I am sure that there is no one who has a father who is also his best...friend as you are mine."[68]

Right now, I'm trying to hold the bow perfectly still as the arrow named Travis is launched into the world. Travis hasn't quite cleared the bow yet, but he will very soon. It seems like just a few moments ago we pulled him out of our quiver, placed him on the string, focused on the target, and drew the bow. My main concern now is not to lose my concentration by getting distracted by anything other than following through as he leaves. For an archer, even the blink of the eye will interrupt the aim. The analogy to faith is well made by novelist Doris Bett, who said faith is "not synonymous with certainty" but "is the decision to keep one's eyes open."

My parents didn't lose their concentration as they released

their four sons. To make sure their "arrows" would clear their bow without being deflected, they went so far as to wait until my youngest brother was settled in his career, and married, before they sold the family house and moved on to their next season of life. It was a great sacrifice, those last few years of waiting, but nothing distracted them from their determination to follow through as their last arrow was launched.

I see now I had radical parents. Until their parenting responsibilities were completed, they were intent on protecting that physical symbol of family roots embodied in the family house where they raised their sons. After the youngest was established in life, they built a house in northern Wisconsin near my father's grandfather's homestead, where they now grow Christmas trees and enjoy the periodic visits of their grandchildren—and one great-grandchild so far.

The unconditional sacrifice my parents made, combined with their faith and trust, was a combination I couldn't resist. They won my heart, as well as my brothers' hearts. This book has flowed directly from their lives. I pray I've communicated what they taught me well and accurately.

The fifth commandment, which is the first commandment dealing with human relationships, is directed at children, including adult children: "Honor your father and your mother, that your days may be long upon the land which the LORD your God is giving you" (Exodus 20:12). These words bind children to parents in a multigenerational community of faith. This command is unique among the Ten Commandments; it's both a promise and a warning. Disrespect for parents is a serious matter, for it also dishonors God.

I've always taken this command seriously. Honor to me

means giving credit, recognition, decoration, deference, and reverence. The practical side of honoring parents includes gratitude for their monetary sacrifice. When I graduated from college, started my career, and began graduate work, I took out a term life insurance policy on myself with my parents designated as the beneficiaries. If I had died, they would have had at least some return on their investment in me. I don't believe they ever knew I did this.

I also committed to sharing my life with them through ongoing communication. I've had a long phone conversation with my parents at least once a week since I left home in 1966. This comes to nearly two thousand phone calls. I've asked for their counsel and considered their advice with all seriousness. I've shared with them just about everything significant in my life. They've known my plans and dreams since the day I left for college. They aren't dictating my life or interfering; I'm simply sharing my story with them as it unfolds. I'm quite independent. I believe the commandment to honor our parents applies after we've grown up and left home as much as, or even more than, when we were children. Only as adults can we fully comprehend what honor means; we then have more appreciation when it's returned to us.

I can see this happening now with my own children, and I trust it will happen for you with yours.

Sometimes we're privileged to see and hear the results of our efforts firsthand. Remember the weeklong family camps I mentioned earlier, that we hosted at our home? Ten families attended; they had made the romance of their children's hearts a priority. Each year's camp was rich with relationship, but one night stands out. It was still and moonlit. Our children, then of high school age, were talking and singing around a campfire as we parents lay in our beds, listening to their conversation and observing a page of their story unfold. We could hear every word they said. They were passionately sharing with each other how to protect a girl's heart. They discussed free will and election. They sang in harmony accompanied by violin and guitar. They discussed making their way into the world—"planting their fields and building their houses." We shed tears of joy that night as we realized we'd reached our highest objective in romancing our children to God—we had won their hearts.

When all our training, discipling, mentoring, shepherding, and romancing is said and done, when our children have outgrown mud puddles next to soccer fields, when we finally release our arrows into the world and watch them fly away into the future toward eternity, there's no higher joy than knowing their trajectory is fixed on Christ. Although there will be nothing then between us and the target but air, our prayers will have the wings to fly with our arrows, even though we may not be around to see all of the flight.

For as long as I can remember, I've been enchanted by the flight of an arrow. I'm still enchanted, because the flight of an arrow is a mystery, and mystery causes me to wonder. The launched arrow is free to fly, to cut through the air into the far-flung future. The risk and danger of the journey into the unknown now draws my attention. I'm enthralled with it, fascinated—spellbound.

John Eldredge wrote about a breakfast table conversation he once had with his son Luke, who asked, "Are there any great adventures anymore? Are there any great battles...are there any dragons?"[69] Like us, children need an adventure to live. In their dreams they wonder: *Are there any adventures left to live? Is there a place reserved for me?* Inside of them burns the desire, the longing to be the hero or the heroine. No one else can be who our child is meant to be. They have the lead role in the script God wrote for them. According to the secular worldview, few adventures remain; the battle is a myth and the dragon is make-believe—just a fairy tale. Scripture says of this world-view, "I have seen all the works that are done under the sun; and indeed, all is vanity and grasping for the wind" (Ecclesiastes 1:14).

The Christian's view is different. We're guaranteed adventure—high adventure—when we walk the way of wisdom, passionately seeking wisdom as a treasure. The hand of God has personally written us into the Larger Story—the great adventure. This is what we were made for. It captures our souls with a transcendent vision beyond our mortal selves. We aren't some kind of gods building our own little kingdoms—we're warriors winning the kingdom of God. This higher purpose will propel our arrows to places beyond our imagination. This is why I'm enchanted by their flight.

"Like arrows in the hand of a warrior, so are the children of one's youth. Happy [blessed] is the man who has his quiver full of them" (Psalm 127:4–5). This passage usually brings to mind the comforting vision of a parent enjoying the pleasures of a full quiver of children and the security they provide in old age. But the context is war—the spiritual conflict of the ages being waged even as you read. The quiver belongs to a warrior whose desire is to obtain as many arrows as possible to shoot into, through, and even behind enemy lines.

To imagine our precious children involved in a direct D day–style spiritual attack, penetrating Satan's stronghold, is startling. To envision them as Special Forces infiltrating the most dangerous territory of all is almost too much to bear. At the beginning of this book I said that Travis, when he stood on stage and was questioned by an audience of parents, was already in college—a balanced arrow, strong and sharp. He was also involved in a daring ministry that has penetrated the front lines of the secular campus culture. He and several other leaders started a church, using the language, music, and philosophy of the campus to take on hearts for Jesus, just as they would do in a foreign country. I can still see Travis on the first Friday night of the school year, singing to thousands of tattooed and pierced bodies in the city square. He's a winsome warrior among the enemy, and sometimes he flies so high and far that I'm uncomfortable and thrilled at the same time. I never bargained for this much drama. But this is the purpose of parenting. Romancing our child's heart is all about lifting our sights above our human vision, to the context of the Larger Story.

Our daughter Heather's flight may have seemed less dramatic on the surface, but it has led her just as deeply into the battle. Only she serves on a different front—one most of us would rather avoid. Heather has a special gift, a rich ministry bringing hope and joy, love and dignity, to the elderly who are overwhelmed with loneliness and despair as they face their last days on earth. She is Jesus in disguise, holding the hands of people as they die, singing to them, comforting them with the warm sunshine of her smile. She gives as Mother Teresa did—not only her care but her heart as well.

And Dawson—well, at the moment he's out on the porch

hammering together a cage for the caterpillars he carried home in his T-shirt. In the morning they'll probably be all over the house, and Karey will have to pick them out of the bread-box. But the Robin Hood days of my childhood have come full circle, and I know Dawson himself is now the arrow balanced on my string. For all of us as parents, the moment when our children are ready to be released comes much sooner than we anticipate. But the quiver is God's, and on His bow they will fly according to His good purpose and pleasure.

Scripture tells us that Jesus loved His own "to the end." He never faltered in His direction or the intensity of His purpose for them, and neither must we. I remember when Dawson shot his arrows on stage—he never wavered in the power of his concentration, and he hit gold. As parents, we too need to keep our focus, to romance his heart every moment so that when we release him he will fly...not only straight and true, but high and far, winning other hearts for Jesus as his has been won, with the Sacred Romance of God's love.

It's up to us not to blink—even if we have to smother our laughs as he digs into his bowl of cereal and says, "I've been thinking about collecting tarantulas—just like you used to...."

The publisher and author would love to hear your comments about this book. *Please contact us at:* www.multnomah.net/monteswan

# Notes

*Prologue: Straight and True*

   1. From the song "Arrows," by Monte Swan.

*Chapter 1: Once upon a Childhood*

   2. Charles Pellegrino, *Unearthing Atlantis: An Archaeological Odyssey* (New York: Random House, Vintage Books, 1993), dedication.

*Chapter 2: Finding the Silver Bullet*

   3. Karey Swan, *Hearth and Home: Recipes for Life* (Sisters, OR: Loyal Publishing, 1996), 167.

   4. Steve Randazzo, "Fairy-Tale Romance." Used by permission.

*Chapter 3: Living the Larger Story*

   5. C. S. Lewis, *The Last Battle* (New York: Macmillan, 1956), 173–174.

   6. *The Collected Works of G. K. Chesterton: Heretics, Orthodoxy, the Blatchford Controversies*, ed. David Dooley (San Francisco: Ignatius Press, 1986), 264.

   7. Brent Curtis and John Eldredge, *The Sacred Romance: Drawing Closer to the Heart of God* (Nashville: Thomas Nelson, 1997), 35.

   8. C. S. Lewis, *The Screwtape Letters* (New York: Macmillan, 1956), 76–77.

   9. Eleanor H. Porter, *Pollyanna* (Boston: L. C. Page and Company, 1913), 149.

   10. John Eldredge, *Wild at Heart: Discovering the Secret of a Man's Soul* (Nashville: Thomas Nelson, 2001), 13.

*Chapter 4: The Dynamics of Story*

11. Marian M. Schoolland, *Marian's Big Book of Bible Stories* (Grand Rapids, MI: Wm. B. Eerdmans Publishing Company, 1951), preface.

12. C. S. Lewis, *On Stories: And Other Essays on Literature*, ed. Walter Hooper (New York: Harcourt Brace and Company, 1982), 47.

13. Joe Wheeler, *Dad in My Heart: A Treasury of Heartwarming Stories About Dads* (Wheaton, IL: Tyndale House Publishers, 1997), xiii–xiv.

14. Norma Livo and Sandra Rietz, *Storytelling: Process and Practice* (Littleton, CO: Libraries Unlimited, 1986), n.p.

15. Gladys Hunt, *Honey for a Child's Heart: The Imaginative Use of Books in Family Life* (Grand Rapids: Zondervan, 1978), 55.

16. C. S. Lewis, *Of Other Worlds*, ed. Walter Hooper (New York: Harcourt Brace Jovanovich, 1975), 24.

17. Frederick Buechner, *Telling the Truth: The Gospel as Tragedy, Comedy & Fairy Tale* (San Francisco: HarperSanFrancisco, 1977), 81, 90.

18. Vigen Guroian, *Tending the Heart of Virtue* (New York: Oxford University Press, 1998), 8, 178.

19. Ibid., 10 (emphasis added).

*Chapter 5: Out-Romancing the Competition*

20. Arnold Burron, *Discipline That Can't Fail: Fundamentals for Christian Parents* (Greeley, CO: Diamond Peak Press, 1999), 30.

21. Edith Schaeffer, *Hidden Art* (Wheaton, IL: Tyndale House, 1971), 213.

*Chapter 6: The Watershed*

22. See the note on this verse in *The New Geneva Study Bible*, ed. R. C. Sproul (Nashville: Thomas Nelson, 1995), 967.

23. Charles R. Swindoll, *You and Your Child* (Nashville: Thomas Nelson, 1977), 19.

24. S. Clark and J. MacRae, "You Can't Make a Heart Love Somebody," from the album by George Strait (Universal City, MCA Records Inc., Victoria Kay Music/B.M.G. Songs/Little Beagle Music, 1994).

25. As quoted by Curtis and Eldredge, *The Sacred Romance*, 137.

26. Philip Yancey, *What's So Amazing About Grace?* (Grand Rapids, MI: Zondervan, 1997), 12, 26.

## Chapter 7: Requirements for Romance

27. David Elkind, *The Hurried Child: Growing Up Too Fast Too Soon* (Reading, MA: Addison-Wesley Publishing Company, 1992), 4.

28. Gary Chapman, *The Five Love Languages* (Chicago: Northfield Publishing, 1995), 38.

29. Dr. James Dobson, *The Strong-Willed Child: Birth Through Adolescence* (Wheaton: Tyndale House, 1982), 76.

30. Michael Martin Murphey and David Hoffner, "Once Upon a Time," from the album *Americana* (Warner Bros. Records, Inc., Timberwolf Music, Inc. and Hoffner Haus Music, 1987).

31. John Nieder, *God, Sex, and Your Child: What You Need to Tell Your Child About Sex* (Nashville: Thomas Nelson, 1988), 46.

32. Michael Medved and Diane Medved, Ph.D., *Saving Childhood: How to Protect Your Children from the National Assault on Innocence* (New York: Zondervan, 1998).

33. Jean Healy, *Endangered Minds: Why Our Children Don't Think—and What We Can Do About It* (New York: Simon and Schuster, 1990), 195–217.

34. From the song, "What Else Matters at All," by Monte Swan.

## Chapter 8: Parental Incarnation

35. *The Heart of George McDonald*, ed. Roland Hein (Wheaton, IL: Harold Shaw, 1994), xii.

*Chapter 9: Profile of a Romancer*

36. *C. S. Lewis: Letters to Children* (New York: Macmillan, 1985), 5.

37. Brad Roberts, "Superman's Song," from the album *The Ghosts That Haunt Me* (Cha-Ching Records, 1991).

38. See Paul C. Vitz, *Faith of the Fatherless: The Psychology of Atheism* (Dallas: Spence Publishing, 1999).

39. C. S. Lewis, *Present Concerns and Other Essays*, ed. Walter Hooper (New York: Harcourt Brace Jovanovich, 1986), 53, as quoted by Terry Lindvall in "Joy and *Sehnsucht*," *Mars Hill Review* 8 (summer 1997):25–38. *Leadership U,* http://www.leaderu.com/marshill/mhr08/hall1.html (accessed 1 May 2003).

40. C. S. Lewis, *Screwtape*, 57–58, as quoted by Terry Lindvall in "Joy and *Sehnsucht*," *Mars Hill Review* 8 (summer 1997):25–38. *Leadership U,* http://www.leaderu.com/marshill/mhr08/hall1.html (accessed 1 May 2003).

41. C. S. Lewis, *They Stand Together: The Letters of C. S. Lewis to Arthur Greeves (1914–1963)*, ed. Walter Hooper (New York: Macmillan, 1979), 311.

42. C. S. Lewis, *Letters of C. S. Lewis*, ed. W. H. Lewis (New York: Harcourt, Brace and World, 1966), 289, as quoted by Terry Lindvall in "Joy and *Sehnsucht*," *Mars Hill Review* 8 (summer 1997):25–38. *Leadership U,* http://www.leaderu.com/marshill/mhr08/hall1.html (accessed 1 May 2003).

43. Terry Lindvall, "Joy and *Sehnsucht*," *Mars Hill Review* 8 (summer 1997):25–38. *Leadership U,* http://www.leaderu.com/marshill/mhr08/hall1.html (accessed 1 May 2003).

44. Michael McLean, "The Curse" and "The Melody Within" from the Feature Films for Families film *Rigoletto* (Salt Lake City, UT: Shining Star Music [ASCAP], 1994).

45. Fyodor Dostoyevsky, *The Gospel in Dostoyevsky—Selections from His Works*, ed. The Bruderhof Foundation (Farmington, PA: The Plough Publishing House, 1998), 3.

46. *The Dialogues of Plato*, trans. B. Jowett, M.A. (New York: Random House, 1937), vol. I, 695–6.

47. Karey Swan, *Hearth and Home*, 188, 191.

*Chapter 10: Methods for Romancers*

48. Saxton Pope, *Hunting with the Bow and Arrow* (New York: G. P. Putnam's Sons, 1923), 66, 73.

49. Richard A. Swenson, M.D., *The Overload Syndrome: Learning to Live Within Your Limits* (Colorado Springs, CO: NavPress, 1998), 18.

50. Jay O'Callahan, verbal communication to author.

51. Livo and Rietz, *Storytelling*, 102–3.

52. Michael Martin Murphy and David Hoffner, "Once Upon a Time" from the album *Americana* (Warner Bros. Records, Inc., Timberwolf Music, Inc. and Hoffner Haus Music, 1987).

53. Healy, *Endangered Minds*, 91, 102–3.

54. S. Dante and C. Dante, "So We Never Got to Paris" from the album *Out of the Gray* (Brentwood, Tennessee: The Sparrow Corporation, 1995).

*Chapter 11: The Sense of Wonder*

55. Cornelis Verhoeven, *The Philosophy of Wonder: An Introduction and Incitement to Philosophy*, trans. Mary Foran (New York: Macmillan, 1972).

56. Mike Starkey, *God, Sex, & the Search for Lost Wonder* (Downers Grove, IL: InterVarsity Press, 1998), 26.

57. Ellen Haroutunian, "A Baptism of Imagination: A Conversation with Peter Kreeft," *Mars Hill Review* 5 (summer 1996): 60.

58. S. Carpenter, "Germs of Endearment—Modern Hygiene's Dirty Tricks: The Clean Life May Throw Off a Delicate Balance in the Immune System," *Science News: The Weekly Newsmagazine of Science* 156 (14 August 14 1999): 108–110.

59. From the song "Fires of His Wonder," by Monte Swan.

*Chapter 12: The Creative Image*

60. Dr. Paul Brand and Philip Yancey, *In His Image* (Grand Rapids: Zondervan, Judith Markham Books, 1984), 20–2.

61. Dorothy L. Sayers, *The Mind of the Maker* (San Francisco: Harper and Row, 1941), 22.

62. Karey Swan, *Hearth and Home*, 22.

*Chapter 13: Creative Domains*

63. Beth Thurow, personal communication to the author.

64. *The Dialogues of Plato*, vol. 1, 796.

*Epilogue: High and Far*

65. Philip Yancey, *Reaching for the Invisible God: What Can We Expect to Find?* (Grand Rapids: Zondervan, 2000), 41.

66. Kathleen Norris, *Amazing Grace: A Vocabulary of Faith* (New York: The Berkley Publishing Group, Penguin Putnam, Riverhead Books, 1998), 63.

67. Dr. Larry Crabb, *Inside Out: Real Change Is Possible—If You're Willing to Start from the Inside Out* (Colorado Springs: NavPress, 1988), 184.

68. Theodore Roosevelt, *A Bully Father: Theodore Roosevelt's Letters to His Children* (New York: Random House, 1995), 7.

69. Eldredge, *Wild at Heart*, 140.

# CRAFT A STRATEGY TO WIN YOUR CHILD'S HEART

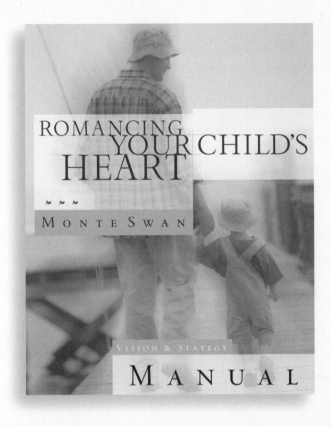

Many parenting books provide formulas to follow for successful parenting, but Monte Swan presents an entirely new approach. Instead of focusing on works, his vision of parenting is based on grace and modeled after the original love story—the gospel of Jesus Christ. This companion to Swan's popular *Romancing Your Child's Heart* coaches both couples and single parents in winning their children's hearts for God, helping them craft a uniquely tailored romance for each of their children. This engaging, fully relationship-focused manual will not only help parents win their children's hearts for God, but will also invigorate and deepen their own relationship with Christ.

ISBN 1-59052-270-2